Mastering

C# 12 .NET Core 8

Building Multi-Platform Applications with C#

Asher Vane

Contents

1. Getting Started with C# 12 and .NET Core 8

1.1 Introduction to the .NET Ecosystem

From developing applications across nearly all conceivable platforms and architectures, Microsoft's .NET has been the ubiquitous framework. It has changed with time from one primarily focused on the development of Windows-centric applications to a versatile, cross-platform ecosystem with the advent of .NET Core. With the latest version of .NET Core 8, Microsoft is pushing the envelope forward on performance, cross-platform compatibility, and developer productivity.

And with the framework came the evolution of C#, which became the first language for .NET. C# 12 is the latest language iteration, providing several enhancements to the language so developers can have cleaner, more maintainable code and increased efficiency. In this chapter, we explore these innovations within the larger context of the broader .NET ecosystem.

1.1.1 Evolution of C# and .NET Core

C# was first introduced back in the early 2000s as part of the original .NET Framework. Developed for combining the power of C++ with the ease of languages such as Java, it has today become the synonym for modern Windows application development.

But this was not for too long, because the need for cross-platform development arose, and Microsoft brought out a light, cross-platform, open-source version of .NET known as .NET Core in 2016. Then, ever since, .NET Core was in direct use to develop applications on Windows, Linux, and macOS and grew to become a totally encompassing .NET 5 and subsequent versions up to .NET Core 8.

Main milestones in .NET:

.NET Framework (2002)	The first Windows-only platform.
. NET Core (2016)	Cross-platform, open-source edition of .NET.
.NET 5 and beyond (2020+)	.NET unified to work the same on all platforms, formally ending .NET Framework and .NET Core.

1.2 Why Upgrade to C# 12 and .NET Core 8?

With every version, Microsoft ships features that closely tie to the problems developers face in the course of contemporary software development. C# 12 and NET Core 8 bring some phenomenal improvements in both performance, language features, security, and productivity.

Some of the key reasons to move forward are: Performance Advantages: Runtime and memory management follow on the same trend of improvement; hence the application offers many more performance advantages compared to the previous run as applied for cloud-native applications. Language Features: Code is easier to write and see with syntactical features added in C# 12. Cross-platform: It supports more platforms, which means it's at cross-points on compatibility among devices. Cloud-native: Improved integration for services like Azure, also supports Docker as well as Kubernetes. 1.3 What's New in C# 12?

Language 12 introduces some language improvements that center on simplifying syntax, increasing flexibility, and improving the developer experience. Let's see some of these new features in action. Now, let's outline some new features with examples.

1.3.1 Primary Constructors for Classes

Earlier, to declare a constructor, you have to define parameters inside the body of the constructor. C# 12 introduced primary constructors which enable you to declare constructor parameters directly in the class declaration. The code has now become much more concise and readable.

Example

In C# 11 and before:

```csharp
public class Person
    {
        public string Name { get; }
        public int Age { get; }


    public Person(string name, int age)
        {
        Name = name;
        Age = age;
        }
    }
```

In C# 12, with primary constructors:

```csharp
public class Person(string name, int age)
{
    public string Name { get; } = name;
    public int Age { get; } = age;
}
```

This feature significantly reduces boilerplate code, making your classes more streamlined.

1.3.2 Improved Pattern Matching

Pattern matching has been evolving since C# 7, and C# 12 enhances this feature with even more powerful capabilities. You can now use new pattern combinators (such as AND and OR) and perform more complex type checks.

Example:

Suppose you have values and would like to categorize them as small, medium or large based on their values.

C# 11

```
int value = 42;
if (value > 0 && value < 10)
{
    Console.WriteLine("Small");
}
else if (value >= 10 && value < 100)
{
    Console.WriteLine("Medium");
}
else
{
    Console.WriteLine("Large");
}
```

In C# 12 with pattern matching

```
int value = 42;
string size = value switch
{
    > 0 and < 10 => "Small",
    >= 10 and < 100 => "Medium",
    _ => "Large"
};
Console.WriteLine(size);
```

This approach is much more expressive and easier to extend as new patterns are introduced.

1.3.3 Collection Expressions

C# 12 introduces collection expressions, a powerful new feature for creating and working with collections in a concise way.

Example:

In earlier versions, one might have defined a list this way:

```
var numbers = new List<int> { 1, 2, 3, 4, 5 };
```

Using collection expressions in C# 12 you can do the same list in less words:

```
var numbers = [1, 2, 3, 4, 5];
```

It makes the code less verbose, easier to create and work with collections.

1.4 What's New in .NET Core 8?

.NET Core 8 contains many performance improvements, API enhancements, and expanded support for platforms. Let's look at some key features in this version.

1.4.1 Performance Optimizations

Performance is one of the greatest reasons to adopt .NET Core 8. From its first release, .NET Core has always had strong roots in high performance, and version 8 stays on the same course. In short, the applications developed over .NET Core 8 are going to run much faster with far fewer resources, thanks to improved garbage collection as well as faster JIT compilation.

For example, in .NET Core 8, the garbage collector (GC) finally brings to light more optimized memory management, especially for large-load scenarios, thus reducing the chances that large memory deallocation will freeze applications.

1.4.2 New APIs and Libraries

There are some new APIs included within .NET Core 8. Most notably, the working with asynchronous programming has improved, but there are also new methods within libraries that are designed to make every day work much more efficient.

For instance, the new cryptographic APIs enhance both performance and security over any encryption and hashing operations.

1.4.3 Greater Support of cross-platform

NET Core 8 extends support to new architectures and goes further in integrating more and more with ARM64 so that the platform becomes more suitable for edge computing and IoT devices.

In addition, further improvements of Docker support and development features for cloud-native applications will make place .NET Core 8 as the best place for implementing microservices and distributed applications in the cloud.

1.5 Getting Started with C# 12 and .NET Core 8

We have already touched upon significant improvements in C# 12 and .NET Core 8. Let's get started installing your development environment and creating a simple application.

1.5.1 Install NET Core 8 SDK and Runtime

To start development with .NET Core 8 you have to download the current SDK and runtime for your environment.

Visit the official page of the website .NET to download your desired version of SDK.

You can now follow the step of installing according to your platform. So, you have download for either Windows, macOS, or Linux.

The installation is confirmed by the command line in the terminal or command prompt:

```
dotnet --version
```

1.5.2 Your first C# 12 program

After installing .NET Core 8, let's create a simple C# 12 console application.

Open a terminal and create a new console project using the .NET CLI:

```
dotnet new console -n HelloCSharp12
```

Navigate to the project directory:

```
cd HelloCSharp12
```

Write a simple "Hello, World!" program in Program.cs:

```
using System;

class Program
{
    static void Main(string[] args)
    {
        Console.WriteLine("Hello, C# 12 and .NET Core 8!");
    }
}
```

Run the application:

```
dotnet run
```

You should see the output:

```
Hello, C# 12 and .NET Core 8!
```

1.6 Conclusion

C# 12 and .NET Core 8 introduce a lot of strong new features and enhancements to make modern application development faster, easier, and more efficient. Improvements in the performance area, new features for the language, and expanded cross-platform capabilities can make a big boost in your productivity and the performance of the applications you create by using these technologies.

The following chapter will further discuss setting up the development environment, essential tools, and building more complex applications using C# 12 and .NET Core 8.

2 Setting Up Your Development Environment

In this chapter, we will walk you through how to set up your environment for developing applications using C# 12 and .NET Core 8. Getting your environment set up correctly is absolutely essential to a pain-free development workflow. We will cover installing software, talk about what the IDEs are, and then create and run your first application.

2.1 Installing .NET Core 8 SDK and Runtime

Let's start with your environment. You need to download and install the .NET SDK and Runtime for .NET Core 8. The SDK contains everything you will need for development, including libraries, compilers, and the CLI. You also need to have the runtime installed in order to run applications built using .NET.

2.1.1 Installing on Windows

To install .NET Core 8 on Windows:

> https://dotnet.microsoft.com/download

1. Download the .NET SDK for .NET 8, paying attention to download the SDK and not just the runtime.

2. Run the installer and then follow its install instructions.

3. After installing, you can verify the install by opening Command Prompt or PowerShell and then using:

   dotnet --version

If installed, it should give out the version you installed, such as 8.0.x.

2.1.2 macOS Installation

Installation of .NET Core 8 on macOS

1. Download the .NET SDK for macOS from the .NET download page.

2. Upon download, double-click the downloaded .pkg file and follow the installation instructions.

3. After installation, you should be able to open Terminal and verify its installation by running:

```
dotnet --version
```

2.1.3 Installation on Linux

The .NET Core 8 SDK is available for several Linux distributions. For Ubuntu, use the following steps:

Open Terminal and run the following commands in order to install .NET Core 8:

```
sudo apt-get update
sudo apt-get install -y dotnet-sdk-8.0
```

After installation, verify the installation by running the following:

```
dotnet --version
```

On other distributions, such as Fedora or CentOS, additional details can be found at the .NET download page.

2.2 Choosing an IDE for C# 12 and .NET Core 8

Once you have the SDK and runtime installed, you'll want to choose an Integrated Development Environment, or IDE, to author, run, and debug your applications. Microsoft has several choices, each appropriate for one type of developer.

2.2.1 Visual Studio

Visual Studio is Microsoft's fully featured IDE, designed for professional developers who are creating complex applications. It provides full C# 12 and .NET Core 8 support, including full-fledged debugging tools, testing and integration as well as collaboration.

How to get started

1. Download Visual Studio from visualstudio.microsoft.com.

2. During setup, select the workloads : .NET desktop development and ASP.NET and web development.

3. After installing, go to Visual Studio, and you're now ready to create C# 12 projects.

2.2.2 Visual Studio Code

Visual Studio Code, or VS Code, is a lightweight, open-source code editor with very broad ranges of extensions, making it very versatile. It happens to be one of the favorite choices for developers who like keeping it simple yet still flexible enough.

To install VS Code:

1. Download Visual Studio Code from code.visualstudio.com.
2. Install the C# extension from the Extensions Marketplace. It provides support for all language features of the C# language, IntelliSense, debugging and project management tools in addition to everything described in the sections above.
3. Install Tool for Extension Authors to automatically control .NET SDK versions.

After installing, you can use it to develop simple or complex C# and .NET Core in VS Code.

2.2.3 Rider from JetBrains

Rider is a cross-platform IDE with great popularity among those developers working in mixed environments. Rider thoroughly integrates its environment with .NET Core, allowing full-fledged support for up to C# 12 as well as various refactoring, debugging, and unit testing features.

1. Rider from JetBrains download. https://www.jetbrains.com/rider/

2. Install the IDE, then install the SDK .NET Core 8 when you are configuring your project.

Rider is a good option if you already use other JetBrains tools, such as IntelliJ or PyCharm.

2.3 Your First C#12 Project

You are now prepared to create your first C#12 project by using the .NET CLI and other IDEs, including Visual Studio or VS Code.

2.3.1 Creating a Project with .NET CLI

The .NET CLI is a really powerful tool that enables you to create, build, and run .NET projects directly from the command line. To create your first project, you will need:

1. Open your Terminal or Command Prompt.

2. Run following command to create new console application. For Windows users it will be:

   dotnet new console -n HelloWorldCSharp12

This command will create new directory called HelloWorldCSharp12 containing the basic structure of a .NET console app.

3. Navigate to the project folder:

cd HelloWorldCSharp12

4. Open this project in your favorite text editor or IDE, such as Visual Studio Code.

code .

5. Program.cs. Here you'll find a simple example of "Hello, World!":

```
using System;

class Program
{
    static void Main(string[] args)
    {
        Console.WriteLine("Hello, C# 12 and .NET Core 8!");
    }
}
```

6. Just run the following command in your terminal:

dotnet run

7. The console output will look as follows:

Hello, C# 12 and .NET Core 8!

2.3.2 Using Visual Studio to Create a Project

This is relatively even easier if you're working within Visual Studio. Here's how you can do that:

1. Open Visual Studio.

2. Select Create a new project from the startup menu.

3. Select Console App and click Next.

4. Type in a name for the project, and select where you would like it to be saved, for example: HelloWorldCSharp12.

5. Set the framework to .NET 8 and click Create.

Visual Studio will create a basic console application for you with a Program.cs file similar to what we created above using the CLI, and you can run your application by pressing F5.

2.3.3 Creating a Project in Visual Studio Code

Once you have created your project with the CLI, open the folder of your project using VS Code:

1. Run:

   Code

2. You need to install the C# extension if you haven't already.

3. Go to the Program.cs file and change it, if necessary. For instance:

   ```
   using System;

   class Program
   {
       static void Main(string[] args)
       {
           Console.WriteLine("Welcome to C# 12 and .NET Core 8 development with VS Code!");
       }
   }
   ```

4. Run the application in the Integrated Terminal in VS Code:

   dotnet run

You should now see the updated output in the terminal:

Welcome to C# 12 and .NET Core 8 development with VS Code!

2.4 Understanding the Project Structure

You now have created your first C# 12 project. Let's take a look at the structure that is created by either the .NET CLI or Visual Studio.

A typical .NET Core 8 console application looks like this:

```
HelloWorldCSharp12
├── HelloWorldCSharp12.csproj
├── Program.cs
└── obj/
```

2.4.1 The .csproj File

The .csproj file is your project file. It contains configuration data for your application, such as the target framework of your project, project dependencies, and build instructions.

An example of the content of HelloWorldCSharp12.csproj might look like this:

```
<Project Sdk="Microsoft.NET.Sdk">
  <PropertyGroup>
    <OutputType>Exe</OutputType>
    <TargetFramework>net8.0</TargetFramework>
  </PropertyGroup>
</Project>
```

This file states that the project is a console application targeting .NET 8.0 (net8.0).

2.4.2 Program.cs

Program.cs is the entry point of your application. The Main method is where execution begins when you run the application. By default, this file contains a simple Console.WriteLine statement, but you can add more code as your application grows.

2.5 Debugging and Running Your Application

Now that you've written some code, it's important to understand how to debug and run your application in different environments.

2.5.1 Running with .NET CLI

To execute your project from the command line:

Open a command prompt in the project folder and run this command:

```
dotnet run
```

This will compile and execute your project in one single step. Any errors will be spat out in the terminal output.

2.5.2 Debugging in Visual Studio

In Visual Studio, you can debug this way

1. Start By Pressing F5, or by clicking on Start Debugging button in toolbar.

2. The application will run in debug mode and allows you to set breakpoints so you can step line-by-line through the code.

To set a breakpoint left-click within the margin next to the line of code where you'd like to suspend execution. And if the application hits that breakpoint, it will suspend and you can inspect variables, step through the code, evaluate expressions.

2.5.3 Debugging in Visual Studio Code

VS Code also provides rich debugging capabilities:

1. Open Program.cs and add a breakpoint by clicking the line number where you want to pause.

2. Click F5 or go to Run > Start Debugging to run your application in debug mode.

3. VS Code will throw the execution at the breakpoint so you can take a closer look at variables, call stacks, and interact with the debugger.

2.6 Summary

This chapter covered the basic steps for setting up your development environment with C# 12 and .NET Core 8, from the installation of the SDK through to the creation of running your first project using an IDE. Knowing about project structure and how to debug applications is basics that will help you through the ongoing complexity of the projects you're building.

In Chapter 11, we will go more in-depth on the main language features of C# 12, moving on to new syntax improvements and how they might help simplify development tasks.

3. C# 12 Core Language Improvements

The advent of C# 12 brings forward a set of new features and syntax improvements designed to make code more concise and expressive along with demanding performance. This chapter will outline the most impactful changes between C# 12 and what it brings into your code to make it more readable and simpler.

We will introduce new language improvements such as Primary Constructors for Classes, enhanced Pattern Matching, and Collection Expressions, as well as many other improvements that will make you more productive.

3.1 Primary Constructors for Classes

Primary Constructors is one of the nice new features in C# 12. Traditionally, constructors are defined in the class body, which creates a lot of duplicated code, especially when initializing properties. Primary constructors eliminate this redundancy by allowing constructor parameters to be declared directly in the class header.

3.1.1 Traditional Constructor Syntax (Pre-C# 12)

Before C# 12, constructors were usually written like this:

```
public class Product
{
    public string Name { get; }
    public decimal Price { get; }

    public Product(string name, decimal price)
    {
        Name = name;
        Price = price;
    }
}
```

It's a good approach, but it quickly becomes littered with boilerplate code for simple property assignments.

3.1.2 Primary Constructor Syntax (C# 12)

With C# 12, you can simplify the above by using primary constructors. Now you can declare constructor parameters directly in the class declaration itself, and then they can be used to directly set properties.

Here is the same class, this time using primary constructors:

```
public class Product(string name, decimal price)
{
    public string Name { get; } = name;
    public decimal Price { get; } = price;
}
```

That cuts down a lot of code you have to write, makes your class definitions much more concise and readable.

3.1.3 Benefits of Primary Constructors

Less Boilerplate: You no longer have to write out boilerplate constructor code when initializing properties.

Cleaner Syntax: Finally, declaring parameters in the class header makes it directly obvious what values the class expects.

Immutability: Properties can readily be set up as read-only (get-only) and initialized in the constructor itself.

3.2 Improved Pattern Matching

The development of pattern matching has been carried on over recent versions of C#. C# 12 continues to make it even stronger. Pattern matching helps you to simplify complex conditional logic and your code becomes more readable by allowing direct matches using values, types, and conditions.

3.2.1 New Patterns in C# 12

C# 12 provides you with some new patterns, like the following ones:

Relational Patterns: Match values by relational operators (+), (>).

Logical Patterns: You may also chain together lots of patterns using the and, or, and not operators.

Collection Patterns: You can match collections (arrays or lists) based on the number and types of elements they contain.

3.2.2 Relational and Logical Patterns

Suppose you want to categorize a score by its value. You used if-else statement or switch expression with simple conditions that you learned earlier than C# 12

In C# 11

```
int score = 85;

string category;
if (score >= 90)
    category = "Excellent";
else if (score >= 75)
    category = "Good";
else
    category = "Needs Improvement";

Console.WriteLine(category);
```

With C# 12's enhanced pattern matching:

```
int score = 85;

string category = score switch
{
    >= 90 => "Excellent",
    >= 75 => "Good",
    _ => "Needs Improvement"
};
```

```
    Console.WriteLine(category);
```

This is more concise, readable and easily extensible.

3.2.3 Example: List Patterns

It provides the capability of list or array matching based on the number of elements they contain and the types and values of those elements.

Assume that you want to determine if a list contains specific values:

```
    int[] numbers = { 1, 2, 3 };

    string result = numbers switch
    {
        [1, 2, 3] => "Exact Match",
        [1, ..] => "Starts with 1",
        [.., 3] => "Ends with 3",
        _ => "No match"
    };

    Console.WriteLine(result);  // Output: "Exact Match"
```

The [1, 2, 3] pattern matches any array with exactly three elements: 1, 2, and 3. The [1, .] pattern matches any array that starts with 1, and [., 3] matches any array that ends with 3.

3.3 Collection Expressions

C# 12 introduces Collection Expressions, a new feature that enables collections to be created in fewer syntactical words. It is especially useful to initialize arrays, lists, and dictionaries.

3.3.1 Simplification of Collection Initialization

Before the current version of C#, their lists initialization in the code required the collection's constructors to be explicitly instantiated, such as:

```
    var numbers = new List<int> { 1, 2, 3, 4, 5 };
```

With collection expressions in C# 12, you can do the same thing in a much more concise form:

```
var numbers = [1, 2, 3, 4, 5];
```

This new syntax reduces verbosity and enhances readability when dealing with complex collections.

3.3.2 Collection Expressions with Dictionaries

You can also use collection expressions with dictionaries that are easier to write.

In C# 11:

```
var dictionary = new Dictionary<string, int>
{
    { "one", 1 },
    { "two", 2 },
    { "three", 3 }
};
```

In C# 12:

```
var dictionary = ["one" => 1, "two" => 2, "three" => 3];
```

The ["key" => value] syntax makes it easy to create and read from dictionaries.

3.4 Default Values for Lambda Parameters

Another important C# 12 feature is the ability to give default values to lambda parameters, which was impossible earlier with versions before it. This, therefore, makes lambda expressions more similar to regular methods in the manner of parameter support.

3.4.1 Lambda Expressions Before C# 12

With versions before C# 12, you were not allowed to use default arguments for lambda expressions, thus you were forced to provide all arguments when calling a lambda expression:

```
Func<int, int, int> sum = (x, y) => x + y;
```

```
int result = sum(5, 3);  // Output: 8
```

3.4.2 Lambda Expressions with Default Parameters in C# 12

In C# 12, you can now also specify default values for lambda parameters, just as you do with regular methods:

```
Func<int, int, int> sum = (x, y = 10) => x + y;

int result1 = sum(5);    // Output: 15 (y defaults to 10)
int result2 = sum(5, 3); // Output: 8 (y is provided as 3)
```

This approach makes lambdas much more flexible and less reliant on overloads or other methods when using default arguments.

3.5 Interpolated Strings Enhancements

Interpolated Strings in C# INTERPOLATED STRINGS Add Expressions to String Literals Make Formatting and Building Dynamic Strings Easy Continuing Improvement: C# 12 extends this with interpolated string handlers providing finer performance control when interpolating strings, especially for performance-critical applications such as logging.

3.5.1 Interpolated Strings in C# 11

As of previous versions of C#, I created an interpolated string like this:

```
string name = "Alice";
int age = 30;

string message = $"Name: {name}, Age: {age}";
Console.WriteLine(message);  // Output: Name: Alice, Age: 30
```

This works well for simple scenarios; otherwise, it does multiple allocations of temporary strings that lead to poor performance in performance-critical applications.

3.5.2 Interpolated String Processors in C# 12

Interpolated String Handlers in C# 12 The developers can override the construction of interpolated strings for performance optimization in particular scenarios such as logging. They make unnecessary string allocations by doing string formatting only when that's necessary.

An interpolated string handler for logging

Here is how you might use an interpolated string handler for logging:

```csharp
public class Logger
{
    public void Log(string message) => Console.WriteLine(message);

    public void Log(string message, params object[] args)
    {
        if (args.Length > 0)
        {
            message = string.Format(message, args);
        }
        Console.WriteLine(message);
    }

    public void LogIfNeeded(bool shouldLog,
    [InterpolatedStringHandlerArgument("shouldLog")] ref LogHandler handler)
    {
        if (shouldLog)
        {
            Log(handler.GetFormattedText());
        }
    }
}

Logger logger = new Logger();
logger.LogIfNeeded(true, $"This log is only formatted if needed: {42}");
```

Using interpolated string handlers forces interpolation to take place only when it is needed for logging, thereby reducing overhead in performance-critical applications.

3.6 Enhanced Null Safety

C# 12 takes null safety further by adding more advanced checks and syntax to assist developers in avoiding common problems using null reference exceptions, which is any developer's most frequent concern during application development.

3.6.1 Nullable Reference Types in C#

Apart from reference types, the other new features in C# 12 are more ways to safely work with nullable values, which was introduced by C# 8: the ability to declare variables that may or may not contain null values.

Example

```
string? name = GetUserName();
Console.WriteLine(name ?? "Unknown User");
```

If GetUserName() returns null, the ?? operator ensures that "Unknown User" is printed instead, thus avoiding a null reference exception.

3.7 Conclusion

C# 12 brings powerful language features that in some ways make some regular things easier to accomplish, the code more readable, as well as improving its performance and safety level. Some of the new features include primary constructors, enhanced pattern matching, collection expressions, interpolated string handlers, among others - all towards increasing the expressiveness and efficiency of C# in modern application development.

In the next chapter, we will cover Object-Oriented Programming in C# 12, classes, inheritance, and interfaces; we will also introduce new features on structs. All this will help you to create robust, maintainable, and scalable applications in .NET Core 8.

4. Deep dive into C# 12 Advanced Object-Oriented Programming

C# is a completely object-oriented programming language. Most basic OOP concepts need to be grasped, as these are what enable the design of scalable, maintainable, and clean applications. This chapter goes deep into OOP concepts within C# 12, including classes, inheritance, interfaces, and records, in addition to most recent enhancements in C# 12 that simplify OOP design and improve performance.

4.1 Classes in C# 12

A class is a template, or blueprint, for creating objects in object-oriented programming. Classes in C# include fields, properties, methods, constructors, and events as examples. They are at the core of object-oriented design in C#.

4.1.1 Declaring a Class

Following is a simple class in C# 12:

```
public class Car
{
    public string Make { get; }
    public string Model { get; }
    public int Year { get; }

    public Car(string make, string model, int year)
    {
        Make = make;
        Model = model;
        Year = year;
    }

    public void Drive()
    {
        Console.WriteLine($"Driving {Make} {Model} of {Year}");
    }
}
```

This code snippet involves:

Properties Make, Model, and Year are states.

The Constructor gives the method of initializing these state properties.

Drive is an action held in a method by the state of Car class

4.1.2 Creating an Instance

You can declare an instance (or object) of the Car class using the new keyword:

```
var myCar = new Car("Toyota", "Camry", 2023);
myCar.Drive();  // Output: Driving Toyota Camry of 2023
```

Here, we instantiated a new Car object with Make "Toyota", Model "Camry", and Year 2023 and then called the Drive method.

4.2 Inheritance in C# 12

Inheritance forms the core of OOP by enabling one class (the derived class) to inherit properties and methods of another class (the base class). This implies code reuse and creates a natural hierarchy of classes.

4.2.1 Creating a Base and Derived Class

We are going to extend our Car class using inheritance. We will create a base class Vehicle, and a derived class Electric Car inheriting from Car.

```
public class Vehicle
{
    public string Make { get; }
    public string Model { get; }

    public Vehicle(string make, string model)
    {
        Make = make;
        Model = model;
    }
```

```csharp
    public virtual void Drive()
    {
        Console.WriteLine($"Driving {Make} {Model}");
    }
}

public class ElectricCar : Vehicle
{
    public int BatteryCapacity { get; }

    public ElectricCar(string make, string model, int batteryCapacity)
        : base(make, model)
    {
        BatteryCapacity = batteryCapacity;
    }

    public override void Drive()
    {
        Console.WriteLine($"Driving {Make} {Model} with {BatteryCapacity} kWh battery.");
    }
}
```

The Vehicle class is a base class with common properties: Make and Model.

The ElectricCar inherits from the Vehicle and adds a new property, BatteryCapacity.

The Drive method of the Vehicle class is declared virtual-so it can be overridden in derived classes. We override it in ElectricCar to give more specific behavior.

4.2.2 Instantiation and Usage of Derived Classes

```csharp
var myTesla = new ElectricCar("Tesla", "Model S", 100);
myTesla.Drive();  // Output: Driving Tesla Model S with 100 kWh battery.
```

The ElectricCar class inherits properties from the Vehicle class: Make and Model, while defining another property called BatteryCapacity. When you call Drive, it invokes the overridden method of the ElectricCar class.

4.3 C# 12 Polymorphism

Polymorphism This capability allows you to treat objects of different classes as if they were instances of a common base class. Polymorphism is particularly useful when you have collections of objects that happen to share the same base type but will have different implementations of a method.

4.3.1 Polymorphism Example.

Let's modify the example above to demonstrate polymorphism:

```
Vehicle myCar = new Car("Ford", "Mustang", 2022);
Vehicle myTesla = new ElectricCar("Tesla", "Model X", 90);

myCar.Drive();   // Output: Driving Ford Mustang
myTesla.Drive(); // Output: Driving Tesla Model X with 90 kWh battery
```

Here, myCar and myTesla are used as Vehicle objects. But when the Drive method is invoked, the correct version of that method for each variant type (Car or ElectricCar) will be called, based on polymorphism.

4.4 Abstract Classes and Methods

An abstract class is a class that cannot be instantiated directly. It can only be used as a base class. Often, an abstract class contains abstract methods, which are methods that must be implemented in derived classes.

4.4.1 Creating an Abstract Class

Let's take the Vehicle class and make it abstract. We will also define an abstract method Start Engine, which must be implemented by any class that inherits from Vehicle.

```
public abstract class Vehicle
{
    public string Make { get; }
    public string Model { get; }
```

```csharp
    public Vehicle(string make, string model)
    {
        Make = make;
        Model = model;
    }

    public abstract void StartEngine();

    public virtual void Drive()
    {
        Console.WriteLine($"Driving {Make} {Model}");
    }
}

public class GasCar : Vehicle
{
    public GasCar(string make, string model) : base(make, model) { }

    public override void StartEngine()
    {
        Console.WriteLine("Starting gas engine...");
    }
}

public class ElectricCar : Vehicle
{
    public ElectricCar(string make, string model) : base(make, model) { }

    public override void StartEngine()
    {
        Console.WriteLine("Starting electric motor...");
    }
}
```

4.4.2 Using Abstract Classes and Methods

You now can declare objects of the derived classes and you now can call the StartEngine method:

```csharp
Vehicle myGasCar = new GasCar("Ford", "F-150");
```

```
Vehicle myElectricCar = new ElectricCar("Tesla", "Model 3");

myGasCar.StartEngine();    // Output: Starting gas engine...
myElectricCar.StartEngine(); // Output: Starting electric motor...
```

Because the class Vehicle only has a common structure, but specific implementations like GasCar and ElectricCar need to provide the method StartEngine,

4.5 Interfaces in C# 12

A way to define a contract that classes should adhere to is an interface. It states what methods and properties a class should implement without offering any implementation. Generally, interfaces are used primarily to achieve loose coupling between components and to allow for polymorphism without inheritance.

4.5.1 Defining and Implementing an Interface

Consider the declaration of an interface IDriveable:

```
public interface IDriveable
{
   void StartEngine();
   void Drive();
}
```

Any class which implements this interface will make available implementations of the StartEngine and Drive methods. Here's how to do that in a class:

```
public class Motorcycle : IDriveable
{
   public string Make { get; }
   public string Model { get; }

   public Motorcycle(string make, string model)
   {
      Make = make;
      Model = model;
   }
```

```csharp
    public void StartEngine()
    {
        Console.WriteLine("Starting motorcycle engine...");
    }

    public void Drive()
    {
        Console.WriteLine($"Riding {Make} {Model}");
    }
}
```

4.5.2 Using Interfaces

Now any object that implements the IDriveable can be used that way without ever knowing its real type:

```csharp
IDriveable myMotorcycle = new Motorcycle("Harley-Davidson", "Street 750");
myMotorcycle.StartEngine();  // Output: Starting motorcycle engine...
myMotorcycle.Drive();        // Output: Riding Harley-Davidson Street 750
```

The employment of interfaces helps to uncouple code from an implementation, so there is more flexibility and higher reusability.

4.6 Records in C# 12

Records is a special type of class in C# 9, optimized for scenarios where you want to have immutability and value-based equality. Records are more of an antidote to classes rather than a complement. Regular classes are conceived primarily to represent behavior, while records are more concerned with representing data. C# 12 moves another step forward toward allowing records and enhances them further when working with data-centric applications.

4.6.1 Defining a Record

The most basic Person record looks like this:

```csharp
public record Person(string FirstName, string LastName);
```

Records will have automatic implementations of:

Value equality two records are equal if their values are equal.

Compact syntax for immutability : properties are immutable by default.

4.6.2 Working with Records

You can declare records, and use them as classes, but with an added bonus:

```
var person1 = new Person("John", "Doe");
var person2 = new Person("John", "Doe");

Console.WriteLine(person1 == person2);  // Output: True
```

For example, person1 and person2 would be regarded as equal, since their values are the same. In contrast, if classes from classes of traditional objects are used, object comparisons would typically use reference equality unless overridden explicitly.

4.6.3 Record Immutability and Copying

A record is immutable by default; its fields cannot be changed after it has been constructed. It is however possible to make a modification of a record using the with-expression:

```
var person3 = person1 with { LastName = "Smith" };
Console.WriteLine(person3);  // Output: Person { FirstName = John, LastName = Smith }
```

This creates a new Person object, copying all values from person1 except for LastName, which is set to "Smith".

4.7 Structs and Performance

Besides classes, C# also provides structs. A struct represents a structure type which is a value type stored directly on the stack rather than on the heap as with classes. Structs are often used in applications where memory allocations must be as minimal as possible. These usually relate to performance-critical applications.

4.7.1 Defining and Using a Struct

Below is a Point struct:

```
public struct Point
{
    public int X { get; }
    public int Y { get; }

    public Point(int x, int y)
    {
        X = x;
        Y = y;
    }

    public void Display()
    {
        Console.WriteLine($"Point({X}, {Y})");
    }
}
```

Unlike classes, structs do not support inheritance but can implement interfaces:

```
Point point = new Point(3, 4);
point.Display(); // Output: Point(3, 4)
```

The structs are very appropriate for simple, light data structures where copying the values is less expensive than referencing the objects located on the heap.

4.8 Conclusion

Advanced Object-Oriented Programming in C# 12 includes classes, inheritance, polymorphism, interfaces, records, and structs. A group of all these tools gives shape to the skeleton that should be used to develop strong, robust, and maintainable applications in .NET Core 8. If you know how to use these tools well, you will achieve flexible architecture, performance will be improved, and cleaner code will be produced.

In the next chapter, we will learn about Asynchronous Programming and Concurrency in C# 12 so that we can see how to build high-performance applications in order to have the ability to handle several tasks at the same time efficiently.

5. Working with .NET Core 8

NET Core 8 is Microsoft's new cross-platform, open-source framework for building high-performance applications. The following chapter will lead you through some of the key features of .NET Core 8, including building console applications and web applications using ASP.NET Core, working with web APIs. Some of the newly introduced features and features that were improved in terms of performance improvement and increased support for platforms also included.

5.1 Understanding the Architecture of .NET Core

The .NET Core framework is modular, lightweight, and optimized for cross-platform development. It has

- The runtime (CoreCLR) that holds the power of running applications
- Base Class Library (BCL), the standard libraries programmers may use
- Language compilers such as C#, F#, and VB.NET
- ASP.NET Core to build new modern web apps and services
- Entity Framework Core to interact with the database

5.1.1 Important Benefits of .NET Core 8

- **Cross-platform :** You can develop applications running across Windows, Linux, and macOS.
- **Performance:** there are quite a number of performance improvements in .NET Core 8, such as improved garbage collection, faster JIT compilation and memory management.
- **Modularity:** develop only the components that are necessary to use, which means you'd get smaller applications.
- **Cloud-optimized:** it is also highly optimized for the cloud-based environment such as Azure and AWS.

5.2 Creating a Console Application with .NET Core 8

Console applications are the least complex applications you can build with .NET Core. They run in the command-line environment and are well suited for small utilities, batch processing or learning the basics of the .NET framework.

5.2.1 Your First Console Application

To make a new console application:

1. Open your terminal or command prompt.

2. Run the following command to create a new console project:

    dotnet new console -n HelloDotNetCore8

This will create a directory called HelloDotNetCore8 with the skeleton structure of a console application.

3. Navigate to the directory:

    cd HelloDotNetCore8

4. Open the file Program.cs. You'll see the default code that writes "Hello, World!" to the console:

```
using System;

class Program
{
    static void Main(string[] args)
    {
        Console.WriteLine("Hello, World!");
    }
}
```

5. To run the application, use the following command:

dotnet run

The output will be

Hello, World!

5.2.2 Improving the Console Application

Let's improve the program so that it takes a user's input and does some arithmetic operations with respect to his/her input:

```
using System;

class Program
{
    static void Main(string[] args)
    {
        Console.WriteLine("Enter the first number:");
        int num1 = Convert.ToInt32(Console.ReadLine());

        Console.WriteLine("Enter the second number:");
        int num2 = Convert.ToInt32(Console.ReadLine());

        Console.WriteLine("Choose an operation (+, -, *, /):");
        char operation = Console.ReadLine()[0];

        int result = operation switch
        {
            '+' => num1 + num2,
            '-' => num1 - num2,
            '*' => num1 * num2,
            '/' when num2 != 0 => num1 / num2,
            '/' => throw new DivideByZeroException("Cannot divide by zero."),
            _ => throw new InvalidOperationException("Invalid operation.")
        };

        Console.WriteLine($"Result: {result}");
    }
}
```

This easy program takes two numbers and performs a user-specified operation. It demonstrates how you can also build interactive console applications with .NET Core 8.

5.3 Creating Web Applications Using ASP.NET Core 8

ASP.NET Core is the web application framework of .NET Core, developed especially for building modern, cloud-based, internet-connected applications. ASP.NET Core is also fast, modular, and cross-platform and is thus good at building APIs, microservices, and web applications.

5.3.1 Creating a Web Application

Let's build a simple web application using ASP.NET Core 8. To get started:

1. Run the following command to create a new web application:

   dotnet new webapp -n WebAppExample

This creates a new ASP.NET Core Razor Pages application.

2. Navigate to the project folder:

   cd WebAppExample

3. Navigate to the project folder:

   dotnet run

Open a browser and go to http://localhost:5000. You will see the default ASP.NET Core template application.

5.3.2 Understanding the Project Structure

Here is the specific structure of an ASP.NET Core project:

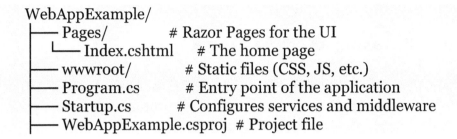

```
WebAppExample/
├── Pages/              # Razor Pages for the UI
│   └── Index.cshtml    # The home page
├── wwwroot/            # Static files (CSS, JS, etc.)
├── Program.cs          # Entry point of the application
├── Startup.cs          # Configures services and middleware
├── WebAppExample.csproj  # Project file
```

Program.cs is the entry point of the application. It creates the host and it initializes the web server.

Startup.cs configures the services and middleware such as routing, authentication, dependency injection for the application.

Pages/ blames Razor Pages for UI logic.

5.3.3 Adding a New Page

In the following example, we add a new page to our application. It is done as follows:

1. Add a new Razor Page:

   dotnet new page -n About

2. You will now notice that there have been created two files: About.cshtml and About.cshtml.cs. Open the file About.cshtml, and there let's add some content:

   ```
   @page
   @model WebAppExample.Pages.AboutModel

   <h1>About Us</h1>
   <p>This is the about page of our .NET Core 8 application.</p>
   ```

3. Add a link to the new page in Pages/Shared/_Layout.cshtml:

   ```
   <li class="nav-item">
     <a class="nav-link text-dark" asp-page="/About">About</a>
   </li>
   ```

Run the application again and navigate to http://localhost:5000/About to view your new page.

5.4 Creating RESTful APIs using ASP.NET Core 8

Using ASP.NET Core 8 makes it incredibly simple to create RESTful APIs. A REST API enables applications to talk to other applications over the HTTP protocol by exposing endpoints that you can use to either retrieve, create, update, or delete data.

5.4.1 Creating a New API Project

To create a new ASP.NET Core API project, you do the following:

1. Run the following command:

    dotnet new webapi -n WebApiExample

This will generate a basic Web API project with a few endpoint defaults.

2. Navigate into the project directory

    cd WebApiExample

3. Run the application

    dotnet run

Open your browser and navigate to http://localhost:5000/swagger. You should see the default Swagger UI, which enables you to play with the API.

5.4.2 Including a Custom API Endpoint

For this task, do the following:

1. Open Controllers/WeatherForecastController.cs. Rename it to ProductsController.cs.

2. Replace existing code with the following code:

    using Microsoft.AspNetCore.Mvc;

```csharp
[ApiController]
[Route("api/[controller]")]
public class ProductsController : ControllerBase
{
    private static readonly List<Product> Products = new()
    {
        new Product { Id = 1, Name = "Laptop", Price = 1000 },
        new Product { Id = 2, Name = "Phone", Price = 500 },
        new Product { Id = 3, Name = "Tablet", Price = 300 }
    };

    [HttpGet]
    public IEnumerable<Product> Get()
    {
        return Products;
    }

    [HttpGet("{id}")]
    public ActionResult<Product> Get(int id)
    {
        var product = Products.FirstOrDefault(p => p.Id == id);
        if (product == null)
        {
            return NotFound();
        }
        return product;
    }

    [HttpPost]
    public ActionResult<Product> Post(Product product)
    {
        product.Id = Products.Count + 1;
        Products.Add(product);
        return CreatedAtAction(nameof(Get), new { id = product.Id }, product);
    }
}

public class Product
{
    public int Id { get; set; }
    public string Name { get; set; }
    public decimal Price { get; set; }
```

```
}
```

3. We now run the application and view http://localhost:5000/api/products. It should return a list of products in JSON format:

```
[
    { "id": 1, "name": "Laptop", "price": 1000 },
    { "id": 2, "name": "Phone", "price": 500 },
    { "id": 3, "name": "Tablet", "price": 300 }
]
```

5.4.3 Testing the API

You can test the API endpoints using applications like Postman or curl. To get a specific product by id = 1, use the following curl command:

```
curl http://localhost:5000/api/products/1
```

To create a new product use POST method:

```
curl -X POST http://localhost:5000/api/products -H "Content-Type: application/json" -d '{"name": "Smartwatch", "price": 200}'
```

5.5 Performance Improvements in .NET Core 8

.NET Core 8 also provides many performance optimizations that make application development significantly faster and more efficient.

5.5.1 Improved Garbage Collection

.NET Core 8 brings improvements in the GC to better manage memory, especially for high-performance applications. Generally speaking, the GC now handles large objects and multi-threaded applications much better than previously, with less memory fragmentation and better performance in long-running services.

C# 12 .NET Core 8

5.5.2 JIT Compilation Improved

.NET Core 8 JIT compiler is faster, so applications start up quicker and runtime performance is improved. Moreover, profile-guided optimizations (PGO) are utilized to optimize the most executed paths.

5.5.3 Native Ahead-Of-Time compilation

Native AOT is a new thing in .NET Core 8where the applications are compiled at build time rather than dynamically at runtime by the JIT. This makes applications much smaller and has very fast startup times especially in microservices and serverless applications.

To use Native AOT in your code, you would simply add this property to your `.csproj` file.

```
<PropertyGroup>
  <PublishAot>true</PublishAot>
</PropertyGroup>
```

Then, publish the application:

```
dotnet publish -c Release
```

This produces a self-contained native executable.

5.6 Conclusion

In this chapter, we have explored the major characteristics of .NET Core 8, such as how to create console applications, web applications with ASP.NET Core, and how to build RESTful APIs. We also discuss performance improvements in .NET Core 8, including better garbage collection and native AOT compilation that makes the framework even more suitable for high-performance and cloud-native applications.

In the next chapter we are moving forward with how to implement data access using Entity Framework Core 8, discussing the basics of using Entity Framework for interaction with databases, performing many common CRUD operations, including creation, reading, updating, and deleting.

6. Accessing Data with Entity Framework Core 8

Interacting with databases is the most common thing being done in modern application development. Entity Framework Core 8 or simply EF Core 8 is the powerful, object-relational mapping tool developed to enable the .NET developer to work with databases in a more abstract, object-oriented fashion rather than just doing loads of SQL queries. It simplifies the access of the database by mapping database tables into .NET objects, thereby allowing users to perform the CRUD actions directly on objects.

This chapter explains how to get started with EF Core 8 and perform common database operations, as well as some advanced features: LINQ queries, Migrations, and async programming for database access.

6.1 Introduction to Entity Framework Core 8

Entity Framework Core is an ORM. Rather than writing raw SQL commands, developers can work with the database using objects written in C#. EF Core works with relational databases such as SQL Server, MySQL, PostgreSQL, SQLite, and many more. It abstracts the data access layer so developers can focus on business logic.

6.1.1 Features of EF Core 8

Cross-platform: Works on Windows, Linux, and macOS.

Async Support: It fully supports async database operations, using async and await.

Migrations: Helps in managing database schema changes with versioning.

LINQ Queries: It supports database queries with Language Integrated Query (LINQ) which improves query readability and maintainability.

Lazy Loading: Related entities in the database are loaded on-demand, while improving performance.

Change Tracking: Automatically track the changes of an object made so that you can persist those changes to the database

6.2 Setting Up EF Core 8

To use EF Core in your .NET Core 8 application you will have to install the required NuGet packages and configure EF Core to work with your database.

6.2.1 Installing EF Core 8

To add EF Core to your project you require the EntityFrameworkCore package, as well as (depending on the database provider) the corresponding provider package-for example, for SQL Server, SQLite, PostgreSQL, and so on.

Let's run the following commands in the .NET CLI to install the required packages for SQL Server:

```
dotnet add package Microsoft.EntityFrameworkCore
dotnet add package Microsoft.EntityFrameworkCore.SqlServer
dotnet add package Microsoft.EntityFrameworkCore.Tools
```

For SQLite, you would use:

```
dotnet add package Microsoft.EntityFrameworkCore.Sqlite
```

6.2.2 Configuring the Database Context

The DbContext class is the heart of EF Core. It corresponds to a session with the database and enables the query and saving of data. Let's create a DbContext for our application.

1. Create a folder called Data within your project.

2. Include a class named AppDbContext.cs :

    ```
    using Microsoft.EntityFrameworkCore;

    public class AppDbContext : DbContext
    {
    ```

```csharp
    public DbSet<Product> Products { get; set; }

    protected override void OnConfiguring(DbContextOptionsBuilder optionsBuilder)
    {

optionsBuilder.UseSqlServer("Server=localhost;Database=ShopDb;Trusted_Connec
tion=True;");
    }
}

    public class Product
    {
        public int Id { get; set; }
        public string Name { get; set; }
        public decimal Price { get; set; }
    }
```

In this class you'll find the following:

- The AppDbContext class inherits from DbContext and refers to the class that is connected to the database.
- Products is a property of type DbSet Product ; that maps Product class to database table.
- The OnConfiguring method is used to declare the connection string to use for SQL Server database.

If you are using SQLite, your OnConfiguring method would look like this:

```csharp
        optionsBuilder.UseSqlite("Data Source=shop.db");
```

6.3 Using Migrations

Migrations in EF Core are used to change the database schema over time incrementally without losing information. They essentially represent SQL scripts that can change the schema controlled.

6.3.1 Your First Migration

Once you have configured your DbContext, you can create the first migration in order to generate the database schema:

Open the terminal and run:

```
dotnet ef migrations add InitialCreate
```

This creates a new migration called InitialCreate. It includes creating the table Products in the database.

6.3.2 Applying the Migration

You will need to use the following command for making the migration, thereby creating the database

```
dotnet ef database update
```

6.3.3 Verify the Database

You can connect to your SQL Server or SQLite database using tools like SQL Server Management Studio (SSMS) or SQLite Browser to verify that the Products table has indeed been created.

6.4 CRUD Operations

The most common database operations are generally referred to as CRUD operations—short for Create, Read, Update, and Delete records. EF Core eliminates overhead by allowing you to perform all CRUD operations directly on objects.

6.4.1 Creating Data (Insert)

To add a new record in the database, instantiate the entity, and then add it to the DbSet. Finally, save the changes.

How to add a new product:

```
using var context = new AppDbContext();
```

```
var newProduct = new Product
{
    Name = "Laptop",
    Price = 1200m
};

context.Products.Add(newProduct);
context.SaveChanges();

Console.WriteLine($"Product added with ID: {newProduct.Id}");
```

In this example

A Product object was created and added to the Products DbSet.

SaveChanges() saves the new product to the database.

6.4.2 Retrieval Reading

To read data from the database, you may use LINQ queries.

How to get all products:

```
using var context = new AppDbContext();

var products = context.Products.ToList();

foreach (var product in products)
{
    Console.WriteLine($"ID: {product.Id}, Name: {product.Name}, Price: {product.Price}");
}
```

You could also filter the data with Where:

```
var expensiveProducts = context.Products
    .Where(p => p.Price > 1000)
    .ToList();

foreach (var product in expensiveProducts)
{
```

```
Console.WriteLine($"Expensive Product: {product.Name} - ${product.Price}");
}
```

6.4.3 Updating Data

In order to update a record, first, you need to get it from the database, then change properties and call SaveChanges():

```
using var context = new AppDbContext();

var product = context.Products.FirstOrDefault(p => p.Id == 1);

if (product != null)
{
    product.Price = 1100m;
    context.SaveChanges();

    Console.WriteLine("Product updated.");
}
```

This code reads a product via Id = 1, changes the price, and writes those changes back to the database.

6.4.4 Deleting Data

A record may be deleted by reading an entity and then removing it from DbSet:

```
using var context = new AppDbContext();

var product = context.Products.FirstOrDefault(p => p.Id == 2);

if (product != null)
{
    context.Products.Remove(product);
    context.SaveChanges();

    Console.WriteLine("Product deleted.");
}
```

This code deletes a product from a database by Id = 2.

6.5 LINQ with Entity Framework Core 8

Language Integrated Query (LINQ) is C#'s powerful query syntax that lets you ask questions of collections, including database tables, in a readable and type-safe way. LINQ plays nicely with EF Core to express your C# queries as SQL calls that the database carries out.

6.5.1 LINQ Basics

LINQ queries can be declared using two equivalent syntaxes: method syntax or query syntax.

Using method syntax to retrieve all products whose price exceeds 500:

```
var products = context.Products
  .Where(p => p.Price > 500)
  .ToList();
```

The same query using query syntax:

```
var products = from p in context.Products
        where p.Price > 500
        select p;

foreach (var product in products)
{
   Console.WriteLine($"{product.Name} - ${product.Price}");
}
```

6.5.2 Sorting and Grouping Data

You can sort and group data using LINQ's OrderBy, ThenBy, and GroupBy methods.

Sorting by price:

```
var sortedProducts = context.Products
```

```
        .OrderBy(p => p.Price)
        .ToList();

    foreach (var product in sortedProducts)
    {
        Console.WriteLine($"{product.Name} - ${product.Price}");
    }
```

Grouping products by price range:

```
    var groupedProducts = context.Products
        .GroupBy(p => p.Price > 1000 ? "Expensive" : "Affordable");

    foreach (var group in groupedProducts)
    {
        Console.WriteLine($"{group.Key}:");

        foreach (var product in group)
        {
            Console.WriteLine($"  {product.Name} - ${product.Price}");
        }
    }
```

6.6 Asynchronous Database Operations

With EF Core, you can have truly asynchronous operation. Your application does not sleep waiting for the database to do its job. Using async and await should make it hard to block any thread that works with the database.

6.6.1 Async CRUD Operations

Using EF Core 8

Create (Insert):

```
    var newProduct = new Product { Name = "Tablet", Price = 300m };
    await context.Products.AddAsync(newProduct);
    await context.SaveChangesAsync();
```

Read (Retrieve)

```
var products = await context.Products.ToListAsync();
```

Update:

```
var product = await context.Products.FirstOrDefaultAsync(p => p.Id == 1);
if (product != null)
{
    product.Price = 950m;
    await context.SaveChangesAsync();
}
```

Delete:

```
var product = await context.Products.FirstOrDefaultAsync(p => p.Id == 1);
if (product != null)
{
    context.Products.Remove(product);
    await context.SaveChangesAsync();
}
```

6.7 Concurrency in EF Core 8

Concurrency is when one user tries to update a record and another user is still attempting to edit the same record. EF Core has mechanisms designed for handling concurrency gracefully so that the consistency of the database is assured.

6.7.1 Optimistic Concurrency Control

Optimistic concurrency makes only a very weak assumption: that true conflicts are extremely rare. EF Core detects the updates done to the same record by multiple users and then throws a DbUpdateConcurrencyException in such cases.

To enable the concurrency control, you need to add a RowVersion property into your model:

```
public class Product
```

```
{
    public int Id { get; set; }
    public string Name { get; set; }
    public decimal Price { get; set; }

    [Timestamp]
    public byte[] RowVersion { get; set; }
}
```

EF Core automatically tracks changes using the RowVersion field. If a concurrency exception is raised while updating, you might want to do something like this:

```
try
{
    await context.SaveChangesAsync();
}
catch (DbUpdateConcurrencyException ex)
{
    Console.WriteLine("Concurrency conflict detected.");
}
```

That way, you can detect and resolve conflicts without losing any of your data.

6.8 Conclusion

During this chapter, you saw how Entity Framework Core 8 may simplify common database operations. We went over the setting up of EF Core, managing database schema changes through migrations and creating, reading, updating, and deleting data. This also touched on some of the more advanced topics: async operations as well as concurrency handling.

This next chapter is on Asynchronous Programming and Concurrency in C# 12, where you will learn much more about building high-performance applications that can handle multiple tasks more than one at a time.

7. Async Programming and Concurrency C# 12

Async programming and concurrency are important components in the development of modern responsive, high performance applications in software development. An application will asynchronously perform other operations while waiting for a long-running task to complete; if multiple operations occur at the same time, then concurrency is enabled. C# 12 builds on already solid async capabilities, so it's going to be easier to write scalable, efficient code.

This chapter will introduce the reader to the basics of async/await, task-based programming, parallelism, and concurrency collections. Common patterns, pitfalls, and how you may fully exploit asynchronous programming with C# 12 will also be addressed.

7.1 Understanding Asynchronous Programming

Asynchronous programming lets methods start doing tasks such as I/O operations and then return so other code can continue its execution without blocking the calling thread. It has the immediate effect of making applications more responsive-for tasks like network calls, database access, and file I/O-with the waiting time for external resources to act.

7.1.1 Synchronous vs. Asynchronous Programming

Let's start with a simple example to understand the difference between synchronous and asynchronous code.

Synchronous Example

In a synchronous program, every action happens in sequence. The program does not begin to run the next action until the previous one is completed:

```
public void ProcessData()
{
```

```csharp
    string data = GetDataFromDatabase();
    Console.WriteLine(data);

    string fileData = ReadFromFile();
    Console.WriteLine(fileData);
}

public string GetDataFromDatabase()
{
    // Simulate database call
    Thread.Sleep(2000);
    return "Database Data";
}

public string ReadFromFile()
{
    // Simulate file read
    Thread.Sleep(1000);
    return "File Data";
}
```

Asynchronous Example

```csharp
public async Task ProcessDataAsync()
{
    string data = await GetDataFromDatabaseAsync();
    Console.WriteLine(data);

    string fileData = await ReadFromFileAsync();
    Console.WriteLine(fileData);
}

public async Task<string> GetDataFromDatabaseAsync()
{
    // Simulate async database call
    await Task.Delay(2000);
    return "Database Data";
}

public async Task<string> ReadFromFileAsync()
{
    // Simulate async file read
```

```
    await Task.Delay(1000);
    return "File Data";
}
```

This can be used in the ProcessDataAsync method where the await keyword is applied to wait asynchronously for any of these tasks. The application remains responsive while waiting and other tasks can continue to run on the same thread.

7.2 Task-Based Asynchronous Pattern (TAP)

C# Introduces the Task-Based Asynchronous Pattern. It uses two main kinds, Task and Task<T>, to represent work, being done. The async and await keywords rely upon this pattern to compose clean and simple asynchronous code.

7.2.1 Returning Tasks from Methods

When you create asynchronous methods, you should return a Task or Task<T> because it lets another method await the result of your method.

Example

```
public async Task<int> PerformLongRunningOperationAsync()
{
    await Task.Delay(3000);  // Simulate a long-running task
    return 42;
}
```

This method returns a Task<int>, meaning that the result of the asynchronous operation will be an integer. The await keyword pauses the method's execution until the task completes, without blocking the thread.

7.2.2 Avoiding async void

Use async void in almost all scenarios, except where it isn't- which is where an async method cannot return a Task. This can cause errors and exceptions to be swallowed. The exception is event handlers because event handlers are permitted to use async void since events don't support a Task return type.

Correct usage (async Task):

```
public async Task ProcessDataAsync()
{
    // Your async logic
}
```

Incorrect usage (async void):

```
public async void ProcessDataAsync()
{
    // Avoid this, except in event handlers
}
```

7.3 Asynchronous Programming and I/O-Bound Operations

I/O-bound operations, such as file access or network calls, are a great fit for asynchronous programming because the main thread can continue performing other operations while waiting for the operation to complete.

7.3.1 Reading from a File Asynchronously
In the example below, we show how to read from a file asynchronously.

```
public async Task ReadFileAsync(string filePath)
{
    using var reader = new StreamReader(filePath);
    string content = await reader.ReadToEndAsync();
    Console.WriteLine(content);
}
```

In this example, ReadToEndAsync() asynchronously reads the contents of a file. The method awaits the result, allowing other tasks to proceed while the file is being read.

7.3.2 Example: Asynchronous Web Request

You can use the HttpClient class to perform asynchronous web requests:

```
public async Task<string> FetchDataFromApiAsync(string uarl)
{
    using var httpClient = new HttpClient();
    string response = await httpClient.GetStringAsync(url);
    return response;
}
```

It is used to fetch data from a web API asynchronously. The GetStringAsync() method initiates an HTTP request and awaits the response without blocking the thread.

7.4 Parallelism in C#12

As such, while asynchronous programming is used for I/O-bound operations, parallelism is employed for CPU-bound operations to be performed concurrently. The .NET Framework provides the Task Parallel Library (TPL) that makes parallel execution of code easier.

7.4.1 Parallel. For and Parallel. Foreach

The Parallel. For and Parallel. Foreach are two of the methods used in parallel execution of code across multiple threads. These are meant to be used on CPU-bound operations that cannot be completed independently.

Example: Parallel. Foreach

```
var numbers = Enumerable.Range(1, 10).ToList();

Parallel.ForEach(numbers, number =>
{
    Console.WriteLine($"Processing {number} on thread
{Thread.CurrentThread.ManagedThreadId}");
```

```
        });
```

In this code, the Parallel.ForEach calls cause the loop body to be executed concurrently for each element in the numbers collection, distributing work across several threads.

7.4.2 Using Task.Run for Parallel Execution

You can use Task.Run to create CPU-bound work that can be run in parallel. For example, assume you need to compute several unrelated things. You can start them all up using Task.WhenAll to run them in parallel together:

```
public async Task RunCalculationsInParallelAsync()
{
    var task1 = Task.Run(() => CalculateFactorial(10));
    var task2 = Task.Run(() => CalculateFibonacci(20));
    var task3 = Task.Run(() => PerformComplexCalculation());

    await Task.WhenAll(task1, task2, task3);

    Console.WriteLine("All calculations completed.");
}

public int CalculateFactorial(int number)
{
    // Factorial calculation logic
    return Enumerable.Range(1, number).Aggregate(1, (a, b) => a * b);
}

public int CalculateFibonacci(int number)
{
    // Fibonacci calculation logic
    return    number    <=    1    ?    number    :    CalculateFibonacci(number   -   1)   +
CalculateFibonacci(number - 2);
}

public int PerformComplexCalculation()
{
    // Simulate complex calculation
    Thread.Sleep(2000);
    return 100;
}
```

Here, three tasks are done in parallel. When all the three tasks are done the program continues.

7.5 Managing Concurrency using Locks and Semaphores

In a multi-threaded environment, many threads can have access to the same resources at the same time, and many bad things such as race conditions and corruption of data may occur. To avoid this, you need to synchronize access to shared resources.

7.5.1 Using lock for Thread Synchronization

The lock statement in C# ensures that at any given time, only one thread can access a critical section of code:

```csharp
private readonly object _lockObject = new object();

public void UpdateSharedResource()
{
   lock (_lockObject)
   {
      // Critical section of code
      Console.WriteLine("Resource updated.");
   }
}
```

While lock is okay for basic thread synchronization SemaphoreSlim offers finer control since multiple specified numbers of threads can be admitted into a critical section at the same time.

Locking up concurrency with SemaphoreSlim

```csharp
private readonly SemaphoreSlim _semaphore = new SemaphoreSlim(3);

public async Task AccessResourceAsync()
{
   await _semaphore.WaitAsync();
   try
   {
```

```
            Console.WriteLine("Resource accessed.");
            await Task.Delay(1000);  // Simulate work
        }
        finally
        {
            _semaphore.Release();
        }
    }
```

So, in this example up to three threads can enter the critical section at the same time. Semaphore blocks other threads until one of threads working in this critical section completes its work releasing a semaphore.

7.6 Concurrent Collections in C#

If you are developing multi-threaded applications, the standard collections, such as List<T> or Dictionary<K, V>, could be corrupted by accessing it concurrently. C# supports concurrent collections. These are collections that are designed for multi-threaded applications and are thread-safe.

7.6.1 ConcurrentDictionary

The ConcurrentDictionary is a class representing a thread-safe dictionary that supports concurrent read and write operation.

Example

```
var dictionary = new ConcurrentDictionary<int, string>();

Parallel.For(0, 10, i =>
{
    dictionary.TryAdd(i, $"Value {i}");
});

foreach (var kvp in dictionary)
{
    Console.WriteLine($"{kvp.Key}: {kvp.Value}");
}
```

In this example, several threads may add items to the ConcurrentDictionary without causing data corruption.

7.6.2 BlockingCollection

The BlockingCollection<T> class is a collection type, which offers thread-safe producer-consumer model-where one or more threads produce items whilst other threads consume them.

Example:

```csharp
var blockingCollection = new BlockingCollection<int>();

// Producer
Task.Run(() =>
{
    for (int i = 0; i < 10; i++)
    {
        blockingCollection.Add(i);
        Console.WriteLine($"Produced: {i}");
        Thread.Sleep(500);
    }
    blockingCollection.CompleteAdding();
});

// Consumer
Task.Run(() =>
{
    foreach (var item in blockingCollection.GetConsumingEnumerable())
    {
        Console.WriteLine($"Consumed: {item}");
    }
}).Wait();
```

In this example, the producer adds elements to the BlockingCollection; the consumer processes them concurrently. CompleteAdding() ensures no elements are added after the producer has finished working on them.

7.7 Best Practices for Asynchronous Programming

There are several best practices when it comes to using asynchronous programming to make your applications efficient and maintainable:

Avoid Blocking Calls: Do not mix synchronous and asynchronous code. Never block on asynchronous operations using .Wait() or .Result; this could dead-lock.

Do not do this

```
var result = GetDataFromApiAsync().Result;  // Avoid blocking with .Result
```

Use await instead:

```
var result = await GetDataFromApiAsync();
```

Use Async All the Way: Once you use async in a method, use async calls all the way down. Mixing async and synchronous code causes performance problems.

Use ConfigureAwait(false): When you use library code, or code that's not on the UI thread, avoid capturing the synchronization context using ConfigureAwait(false). This will prevent unnecessary context switching, which improves performance.

Example:

```
await Task.Delay(1000).ConfigureAwait(false);
```

Handle Exceptions: Ensure any exceptions that are thrown from an async method are caught and dealt with. Uncaught exceptions in an async method will crash the application.

Example:

```
try
```

```
    {
        await SomeAsyncOperation();
    }
    catch (Exception ex)
    {
        Console.WriteLine($"Error: {ex.Message}");
    }
```

7.8 Conclusion

You learned in this chapter the basic concepts of asynchronous programming and concurrency in C# 12 and went through topics such as async/await pattern, task-based programming, handling both I/O-bound and CPU-bound tasks, and how to do it effectively and efficiently. Other topics included parallelism, thread synchronization using lock and SemaphoreSlim, and concurrent collections such as ConcurrentDictionary and BlockingCollection. All this can be used in the building of applications that are responsive, scalable, and high-performance, making resource and task management smooth and efficient.

In the next chapter, we are going to cover Modern Web Development using ASP.NET Core 8, in which we will go deep into building REST APIs, real-time applications using SignalR, and web applications using Blazor.

8. Modern Web Development with ASP.NET Core 8

ASP.NET Core 8 is the mighty framework for modern web and API development. The features and libraries available provide ways to build dynamic high-performance applications that can be used on any platform. Here's how to start your journey with building a basic web application using ASP.NET Core 8 by taking you through creating an MVC application, building a REST API, and real time functionality with SignalR. We'll also introduce you to the fundamentals of Blazor - a framework for developing dynamic web UIs with the aid of C# programming.

8.1 Overview to ASP.NET Core 8

ASP.NET Core 8 is an open-source, cross-platform framework developed for the building of web applications and services. Here are some of the prominent features:

MVC Framework: Model-View-Controller pattern for structured, maintainable web applications

Razor Pages: Lightweight way of structuring web pages with support for server-side logic

REST APIs: Basic support for developing JSON-based web APIs.

SignalR: A library adding real-time functionality to apps.

Blazor: A web framework for building interactive, client-side UI with C#.

ASP.NET Core 8 brings performance and productivity improvements and new features across the board, and there are improvements in all things related to cloud and microservices-based architectures.

8.2 Creating an ASP.NET Core MVC Application

The MVC is one of the most frequently used patterns to structure a web application. The ASP.NET Core MVC framework breaks an application into three connected, independent components:

Model: This is where the data and business logic are represented.

View: The view is where data is presented to the user.

Controller: This controller captures the user's input and retrieves data from a given source, then it may update the view.

8.2.1 Creating a New MVC Application

To create a new MVC application in ASP.NET Core run the following command on the terminal.

```
dotnet new mvc -n MyMvcApp
```

Now navigate to the newly created project directory.

```
cd MyMvcApp
```

Running the application.

```
dotnet run
```

Navigate to http://localhost:5000 in your browser, and you will be viewing the default MVC template in action.

8.2.2 Project Structure

An ASP.NET Core MVC project includes a predefined folder structure as shown below:

```
MyMvcApp/
├── Controllers/    # Contains controllers (e.g., HomeController.cs)
├── Models/         # Contains model classes (e.g., Product.cs)
├── Views/          # Contains views (e.g., Home/Index.cshtml)
├── wwwroot/        # Contains static files (CSS, JS, images)
```

```
├── Program.cs        # Configures and runs the application
├── Startup.cs        # Configures services and middleware
├── appsettings.json  # Configuration file
```

8.2.3 Create a Controller and View

Let's create a simple page to list products.

1. **Create a Product Model:** In the Models folder, add a Product.cs file:

    ```csharp
    public class Product
    {
        public int Id { get; set; }
        public string Name { get; set; }
        public decimal Price { get; set; }
    }
    ```

2. **Add a Product Controller:** In the Controllers folder, add a ProductController.cs file:

    ```csharp
    using Microsoft.AspNetCore.Mvc;
    using MyMvcApp.Models;
    using System.Collections.Generic;

    public class ProductController : Controller
    {
        public IActionResult Index()
        {
            var products = new List<Product>
            {
                new Product { Id = 1, Name = "Laptop", Price = 1000 },
                new Product { Id = 2, Name = "Phone", Price = 500 },
                new Product { Id = 3, Name = "Tablet", Price = 300 }
            };
            return View(products);
        }
    }
    ```

3. **Create a View for the Product Page:** In the Views/Product folder, add an Index.cshtml file:

```
@model IEnumerable<MyMvcApp.Models.Product>

<h2>Product List</h2>
<table>
  <tr>
    <th>Name</th>
    <th>Price</th>
  </tr>
  @foreach (var product in Model)
  {
    <tr>
      <td>@product.Name</td>
      <td>@product.Price</td>
    </tr>
  }
</table>
```

4. **Run the Application:** Start the application and navigate to http://localhost:5000/Product to see the list of products.

8.3 Building REST APIs with ASP.NET Core 8

With ASP.NET Core 8, developing RESTful APIs is rather easy; your application may actually expose data in a manner that would be consumed by other applications.

8.3.1 Create A New Web API Project

Let's create a new Web API project using this command:

```
dotnet new webapi -n MyApiApp
```

Navigate to the directory where the new project is located. Run the application

```
cd MyApiApp
dotnet run
```

8.3.2. Add a Simple Product API

1. **Product Model:** Within the Models folder, you create the file Product.cs:


```
public class Product
{
    public int Id { get; set; }
    public string Name { get; set; }
    public decimal Price { get; set; }
}
```


2. **Add a Product Controller:** The controllers folder gets added by
    ProductController.cs

```
using Microsoft.AspNetCore.Mvc;
using MyApiApp.Models;
using System.Collections.Generic;

[Route("api/[controller]")]
[ApiController]
public class ProductController : ControllerBase
{
    private static readonly List<Product> Products = new List<Product>
    {
        new Product { Id = 1, Name = "Laptop", Price = 1000 },
        new Product { Id = 2, Name = "Phone", Price = 500 },
        new Product { Id = 3, Name = "Tablet", Price = 300 }
    };

    [HttpGet]
    public ActionResult<IEnumerable<Product>> GetProducts()
    {
        return Products;
    }
}
```

```csharp
[HttpGet("{id}")]
public ActionResult<Product> GetProduct(int id)
{
    var product = Products.Find(p => p.Id == id);
    if (product == null)
        return NotFound();
    return product;
}
}
```

3. **Testing the API:** Run the application and navigate to http://localhost:5000/api/Product in your browser or use Postman to test the endpoints. It will return the list of products as JSON.

8.3.3 API Documentation Using Swagger

ASP.NET Core comes with Swagger, which is an API documentation tool. Swagger allows for easy exploration and testing of your API.

1. Install the **Swashbuckle.AspNetCore** package

    ```
    dotnet add package Swashbuckle.AspNetCore
    ```

2. Configure Swagger in Program.cs:

    ```csharp
    builder.Services.AddSwaggerGen();
    var app = builder.Build();
    app.UseSwagger();
    app.UseSwaggerUI();
    ```

3. Run the application, and navigate to the Swagger documentation. Explore your API by accessing http://localhost:5000/swagger.

8.4 Real-time Functionality with SignalR

SignalR is a library part of ASP.NET Core, adding real-time web functionality to applications. It lets you easily add real-time web functionality to applications such as live updates, notification and activity feeds, and live dashboards for weather forecasts, stock prices, etc.

8.4.1 Including SignalR

The easiest part is including SignalR by installing the package through the terminal using the following command:

```
dotnet add package Microsoft.AspNetCore.SignalR
```

8.4.2 Creating a SignalR Hub

A Hub is just a class that is intended to manage client connections and groups, as well as its messaging.

1. Inside your project, create the file: ChatHub.cs:

```csharp
using Microsoft.AspNetCore.SignalR;
using System.Threading.Tasks;

public class ChatHub : Hub
{
    public async Task SendMessage(string user, string message)
    {
        await Clients.All.SendAsync("ReceiveMessage", user, message);
    }
}
```

2. Configure SignalR in Program.cs:

```csharp
var builder = WebApplication.CreateBuilder(args);
builder.Services.AddSignalR();
var app = builder.Build();

app.UseRouting();
app.MapHub<ChatHub>("/chatHub");
app.Run();
```

3. Creating the Client-Side Chat UI: In wwwroot, create a simple HTML page to test SignalR.

```html
<!DOCTYPE html>
<html>
<head>
  <title>Chat</title>
  <script src="https://cdnjs.cloudflare.com/ajax/libs/microsoft-signalr/5.0.11/signalr.min.js"></script>
</head>
<body>
  <input type="text" id="user" placeholder="Enter your name" />
  <input type="text" id="message" placeholder="Enter message" />
  <button onclick="sendMessage()">Send</button>
  <ul id="messagesList"></ul>

  <script>
    const connection = new signalR.HubConnectionBuilder()
      .withUrl("/chatHub")
      .build();

    connection.on("ReceiveMessage", (user, message) => {
      const msg = document.createElement("li");
      msg.textContent = `${user}: ${message}`;
      document.getElementById("messagesList").appendChild(msg);
    });

    connection.start().catch(err => console.error(err.toString()));

    function sendMessage() {
      const user = document.getElementById("user").value;
      const message = document.getElementById("message").value;
      connection.invoke("SendMessage", user, message).catch(err =>
console.error(err.toString()));
    }
  </script>
</body>
</html>
```

This is an HTML page that configures a SignalR client and connects it to the /chatHub endpoint. It posts messages to the hub and displays the received messages in real time.

8.5 Building Web UIs with Blazor

Blazor is a framework that allows you to build interactive web UIs using C#. You can create a client-side application with.NET, thereby avoiding JavaScript for many cases.

8.5.1 Setting up a Blazor Project

To create a new Blazor Server project, run the following command in your terminal:

```
dotnet new blazorserver -n BlazorApp
```

Navigate to the project directory and run the application:

```
cd BlazorApp
dotnet run
```

8.5.2 Creating a Blazor Component

Blazor uses components, which are reusable building blocks for the UI.

1. In the Pages folder, create a CounterComponent.razor file:

```
@page "/counter"
<h3>Counter</h3>
<p>Current count: @count</p>
<button @onclick="IncrementCount">Click me</button>

@code {
    private int count = 0;

    private void IncrementCount()
    {
        count++;
    }
}
```

This component defines a button that increments a counter. The @code block holds the component's logic.

2. To use the component, add a link to it in Shared/NavMenu.razor:

```
<a href="counter">Counter</a>
```

When you navigate to http://localhost:5000/counter, you'll see the counter component with an interactive button.

8.6 Conclusion

We had the major concepts of ASP.NET Core 8 used in building web applications. These include basic MVC application setup, building a RESTful API, and the incorporation of real-time functionality by using SignalR, with Blazor used for developing interactive web UIs based on C#. All these will be serving to give all that is required to produce powerful, scalable, and responsive web applications.

In the following chapter, we test and debug using C# 12 and .NET Core 8. Unit testing best practices include integration testing best practices along with debugging techniques to make your code high quality and maintainable.

9. Testing and Debugging with C# 12 and.NET Core 8

It is not only about features but also that they work the way they should while writing robust and maintainable code. It is by testing the code that you can check if the developed code is correct. Developers can find where things might be going wrong through debugging techniques. This chapter explains good practices on unit testing, integration testing, in relation to C# 12 with.NET Core 8, as well as ways of debugging effectively.

9.1 Introduction to Unit Testing

Unit Testing is the testing of small units of code, for example, functions or methods, to make sure that they work in isolation correctly. Unit tests are generally automated, quick to run, and independent of each other.

9.1.1 Advantages of Unit Testing

Error Prevention: Identifies problems at an early stage of development.

Refactoring Safety: Ensures that changes don't bring bugs into the existing code.

Documentation: Unit tests describe what a unit of code ought to do.

Regression Testing: Acts as a safety net around code changes.

9.2 Installing xUnit to Perform Unit Testing

xUnit is a popular open-source.NET testing library that is light, extensible, and designed to use with.NET Core. It can also be used with other.NET libraries for testing, like NUnit and MSTest.

9.2.1 Installing xUnit

To add xUnit to your.NET project, you use the following command:

```
dotnet add package xunit
dotnet add package Microsoft.NET.Test.Sdk
```

```
dotnet add package xunit.runner.visualstudio
```

This installs xUnit, the.NET test SDK, and the xUnit runner for Visual Studio.

9.2.2 Creating a Test Project

To create a test project for your existing.NET application, you use the following steps:

1. Create a new test project in the solution:

    ```
    dotnet new xunit -n MyApp.Tests
    ```

2. Add a project reference to the application you wish to test:

    ```
    dotnet add MyApp.Tests/MyApp.Tests.csproj reference MyApp/MyApp.csproj
    ```

You are now ready to start writing unit tests in the MyApp.Tests project.

9.3 Writing Unit Tests with xUnit

Create a simple class and begin to write unit tests against it.

9.3.1 Example Class to Test

In the main application project (MyApp), add a Calculator class that contains basic arithmetic methods:

```
public class Calculator
{
    public int Add(int a, int b) => a + b;
    public int Subtract(int a, int b) => a - b;
    public int Multiply(int a, int b) => a * b;
    public int Divide(int a, int b) => b != 0 ? a / b : throw new DivideByZeroException();
}
```

9.3.2 Writing Unit Tests for the Calculator Class

In the test project (MyApp.Tests), add a class called CalculatorTests:

```
using Xunit;
using MyApp;

public class CalculatorTests
{
    private readonly Calculator _calculator;

    public CalculatorTests()
    {
        _calculator = new Calculator();
    }

    [Fact]
    public void Add_ShouldReturnCorrectSum()
    {
        int result = _calculator.Add(2, 3);
        Assert.Equal(5, result);
    }

    [Fact]
    public void Subtract_ShouldReturnCorrectDifference()
    {
        int result = _calculator.Subtract(5, 3);
        Assert.Equal(2, result);
    }

    [Fact]
    public void Multiply_ShouldReturnCorrectProduct()
    {
        int result = _calculator.Multiply(4, 3);
        Assert.Equal(12, result);
    }

    [Fact]
    public void Divide_ShouldReturnCorrectQuotient()
    {
        int result = _calculator.Divide(10, 2);
```

```
        Assert.Equal(5, result);
    }

    [Fact]
    public void Divide_ShouldThrowDivideByZeroException()
    {
        Assert.Throws<DivideByZeroException>(() => _calculator.Divide(10, 0));
    }
}
```

In this example:

[Fact] attribute is used to define a test method.

Assert.Equal checks if the expected and actual values are equal.

Assert.Throws verifies that a specific exception is thrown.

9.4 Running and Analyzing Test Results

To run tests from the command line, you use a command like this:

```
dotnet test
```

This command compiles all tests in a test project and runs them. All the results appear in the console, marking each test as passed or failed.

Alternatively, you can run the tests in **Visual Studio** with the option **Test > Run All** Tests. Visual Studio will provide you with a graphical view of the results.

9.5 Parameterized Tests

Parameterized tests enable you to execute the same test logic on different sets of data. This is helpful when testing different scenarios without writing methods for each case separately.

9.5.1 Using [Theory] and [InlineData]

In xUnit, you have used the **[Theory]** attribute to mark a test as parameterized, and **[InlineData]** to feed in test data.

Example

```
[Theory]
[InlineData(2, 3, 5)]
[InlineData(-1, 1, 0)]
[InlineData(10, 5, 15)]
public void Add_ShouldReturnCorrectSum(int a, int b, int expected)
{
    int result = _calculator.Add(a, b);
    Assert.Equal(expected, result);
}
```

This test method will run three times using different values for a, b, and expected. Each data set verifies correctness for the Add method in a different input.

9.6 Integration Testing

Unit tests test software components in isolation, and **integration tests** verify the interactions between otherwise independent parts of an application. For a.NET Core web application, integration testing often involves API endpoints in the application under test.

9.6.1 Creating an Integration Test for a Web API

As we did when testing API endpoints, let's get started by creating an ASP.NET Core application with its integration test project.

1. Create an xUnit test project.

   dotnet new xunit -n MyApiApp.IntegrationTests

2. Add project references to both the web project and **Microsoft.AspNetCore.Mvc.Testing:**

```
dotnet add MyApiApp.IntegrationTests/MyApiApp.IntegrationTests.csproj reference
MyApiApp/MyApiApp.csproj
dotnet add package Microsoft.AspNetCore.Mvc.Testing
```

9.6.2 Writing an Integration Test for the API

Create a **ProductControllerTests** class in the integration test project:

```
using System.Net.Http;
using System.Threading.Tasks;
using Xunit;
using MyApiApp;
using Microsoft.AspNetCore.Mvc.Testing;

public                class                ProductControllerTests           :
IClassFixture<WebApplicationFactory<Startup>>
{
    private readonly HttpClient _client;

    public ProductControllerTests(WebApplicationFactory<Startup> factory)
    {
        _client = factory.CreateClient();
    }

    [Fact]
    public async Task GetProducts_ShouldReturnOkStatus()
    {
        var response = await _client.GetAsync("/api/Product");
        response.EnsureSuccessStatusCode();

        Assert.Equal(System.Net.HttpStatusCode.OK, response.StatusCode);
    }
}
```

The test server is configured by the **Startup** instance using
IClassFixture<WebApplicationFactory<Startup>>.

The HTTP client creation is facilitated by **CreateClient**.

A GET request to the **/api/Product** endpoint is issued using **GetAsync**, while the response
status is validated as 200 OK through **EnsureSuccessStatusCode**.

Running integration tests will be completed by **dotnet test** for testing whether API endpoints function as expected.

9.7 Debugging Techniques in Visual Studio

Debugging is one of the critical skills you have to understand for debugging the code to be able to identify where problems exist. Visual Studio gives you good debugging capabilities. You are able to step through your code, view the values in variables, and trace over issues in the code.

9.7.1 Setting Breakpoints

A breakpoint is the line at which you pause the execution so that you can look inside the program state.

Setting a breakpoint

1. You simply click on the left-hand margin at the point on the line where you would like the program to pause.
2. Run the application in debug mode. **F5** in **Visual Studio**.
3. The debugger is suspended at the breakpoint allowing you to view the variables in question.

9.7.2 The Watch and Immediate Windows

Watch Window: It enables viewing variable values during the lifetime of a debugging session

Insert a variable into the watch window

Right-click over a variable you wish to be shown in the Watch Window, and select **Add Watch**.

Immediate Window: The Immediate Window allows the writing of code snippets while being debugged and execution evaluation.

View Open the Immediate window Other windows immediately Enter any expressions or statements to run them immediately as soon as you press the Enter key.

9.7.3 Step Into, Step Over and Step Out

Step Into (F11): Enters a function call to debug it line-by-line.

Step Over (F10): Skips over a function call and executes it without entering it.

Step Out (Shift+F11): Exits the current function and returns to the calling function.

This will allow you to step through your code running and also help you troubleshoot issues with methods or calls to functions.

9.8 Logging for Debugging

Logging gives you insight into an application's runtime behavior, tracing problems that may occur during debugging, which could be masked over.

9.8.1 Configuration of Logging in ASP.NET Core

ASP.NET Core provides a built-in logging system that can be configured to write log messages to various output destinations, such as the console, files, or third-party log services.

Example: Console Logging

In Program.cs, configure logging services:

```
var builder = WebApplication.CreateBuilder(args);
builder.Logging.AddConsole();
var app = builder.Build();
```

Example: Using a Logger in a Controller

Inject ILogger into a controller:

```csharp
using Microsoft.AspNetCore.Mvc;
using Microsoft.Extensions.Logging;

public class ProductController : ControllerBase
{
    private readonly ILogger<ProductController> _logger;

    public ProductController(ILogger<ProductController> logger)
    {
        _logger = logger;
    }

    [HttpGet]
    public IActionResult GetProducts()
    {
        _logger.LogInformation("Retrieving all products.");
        return Ok(new[] { "Laptop", "Tablet", "Phone" });
    }
}
```

Run the application, and log messages will appear in the console-very useful in understanding the flow and state of the application.

9.9 Best Practices for Testing and Debugging

Write Isolated Unit Tests: Do not make your unit tests dependent on external resources, such as databases or file systems.

Use Mocking for Dependencies: Use tools like Moq to mock the dependencies used inside the unit test.

```csharp
var mockRepository = new Mock<IProductRepository>();
mockRepository.Setup(repo => repo.GetProducts()).Returns(new List<Product> {
new Product { Name = "Laptop" } });
```

Write Integration Tests for High Value Endpoints: Have integration tests cover your high-value endpoints and external integrations.

Use Logging Everywhere: Utilize logging throughout your application. This will help trace through application issues much easier.

Have Code Coverage: Take advantages of code coverage in the Visual Studio to ensure test covers the critical paths of application.

9.10 Conclusions

Testing and debugging are essential skills for ensuring that software applications are stable and reliable. In this chapter, we discussed **unit testing and integration testing** with xUnit, how to write parameterized tests, and techniques for debugging code in Visual Studio. We have also covered best practices in terms of how to set up logs and how to use mocks to test dependency relationships. All these practices will help you catch things early, improve code quality, and make maintenance much easier.

In the next chapter, we will dive into **Cloud-Native Development with.NET Core 8,** covering the ways to deploy applications to the cloud, integrate with cloud services, and scale applications.

10. Cloud-Native Development using.NET Core 8

Modern application deployment and design lead because of the shift of the trend in computing toward **cloud-based platforms and microservices architecture**. Cloud-native development underlines the development of applications that are scalable, and resilient, so it is possible to run well in distributed cloud-based environments. The built-in support provided by.NET Core 8 for Docker, Microservices, and serverless computing enables developers to be able to fully realize the power of the cloud.

This chapter will cover essential things about cloud-native development using.**NET Core 8**; that is, it shall discuss deploying applications into the cloud, working with **containers, and using serverless functions.** We'll go ahead to discuss **Azure, AWS, and Kubernetes** usage in deploying, scaling, and managing.NET applications effectively.

10.1 What is Cloud-Native Development?

Cloud-native development is a design approach where one uses the cloud elasticity and distributed nature for application building that are

Scalable: Scaling up or down dynamically in response to changes in demand.

Resilient: Can handle failures without affecting the end-users.

Distributed: Spread across more than one server or even multiple regions of a cloud.

Managed: Utilize automated tools for deployment, monitoring, and scaling.

Microservices, containers, and serverless functions allow cloud-native applications to run across multiple kinds of cloud environments and dynamically scale with changes in workloads.

10.2 Configuring Cloud-Native Development with Docker

Docker is a containerization utility, where applications and their dependencies get bundled into a single portable unit. Containers give each application an isolated runtime, thus making applications more repeatable and easier to deploy.

10.2.1. Dockerizing a.NET Core 8 Application

Create a simple web.NET Core 8 API with a Docker container

Begin by creating a simple Docker container for a web-based.NET Core 8 API.

1. Create a web API project

   ```
   dotnet new webapi -n MyCloudApp
   ```

2. Add a Docker file

In the project's root directory, add the Docker file:

```
# Use the .NET 8 SDK as a build environment
FROM mcr.microsoft.com/dotnet/sdk:8.0 AS build
WORKDIR /app

# Copy and build the application
COPY . .
RUN dotnet publish -c Release -o out

# Use a runtime image for the final container
FROM mcr.microsoft.com/dotnet/aspnet:8.0
WORKDIR /app
COPY --from=build /app/out .

# Expose port 80
EXPOSE 80
ENTRYPOINT ["dotnet", "MyCloudApp.dll"]
```

3. Build the docker image

Use the following command to build the Docker image:

```
docker build -t mycloudapp .
```

4. Run the Docker Container

Start the container with:

```
docker run -p 8080:80 mycloudapp
```

The application can be accessed at **http://localhost:8080**.

10.2.2 Multiservice Using Docker Compose

Docker Compose is a tool for writing the definition of a Docker application using YAML. That way, you would define services, networks, and volumes in an overall file.

Example : Docker Compose File – docker-compose.yml

There are two services, a.NET Core API service along with a MongoDB database

```
version: '3.8'
services:
 webapi:
  image: mycloudapp
  build:
   context: .
  ports:
   - "8080:80"
  depends_on:
   - db

 db:
  image: mongo
  environment:
   MONGO_INITDB_ROOT_USERNAME: root
   MONGO_INITDB_ROOT_PASSWORD: example
  ports:
   - "27017:27017"
```

Run the application with:

```
docker-compose up
```

This can start the API and the MongoDB service and allows easier testing of multi-container applications locally.

10.3 Publishing of.NET Core 8 Applications to Azure

.NET Core offers various approaches to publish to Azure like **App Service, Azure Kubernetes Service (AKS)** and **serverless using the Azure Functions**

10.3.1 Publishing using App Service

Azure App Service is a fully managed platform for web applications, APIs, or mobile backends. Automatic scaling happens based on demand and built-in monitoring and logging are available.

1. **Creating a new App Service on Azure**

   - Open the **Azure Portal** > **App Services**.
   - Clicking on **Create** > subscription resource group > region.
   - Runtime stack: **Code** as well as **ASP.NET Core 8**

2. **Deploy from Visual Studio**

   There are built-in support in Visual Studio to deploy.NET applications directly to Azure:

   - Double-click **Solution Explorer** and choose **Publish**
   - Select the appropriate publish target as **Azure** along with your App Service.
   - Click **Publish** to deploy

Once deployed, the deployed application is available on provided Azure URL

10.3.2 Deploy from Azure CLI

If command line is your preference; you can use the **CLI for Azure**:

1. Login into Azure

   az login

2. Create a Resource Group

   az group create --name MyResourceGroup --location eastus

3. Create an App Service Plan

   az appservice plan create --name MyAppServicePlan --resource-group
   MyResourceGroup --sku B1

4. Create a Web App

   az webapp create --resource-group MyResourceGroup --plan MyAppServicePlan --
   name MyUniqueAppName --runtime "DOTNET|8.0"

5. Deploy the App

   az webapp up --name MyUniqueAppName --resource-group MyResourceGroup

Your application will be deployed to Azure and accessible at
https://MyUniqueAppName.azurewebsites.net.

10.4 Microservices with.NET Core and Kubernetes

Kubernetes is an open-source system for automating deployment, scaling and managing
containerized applications. It is widely used in the **microservices architectures**.

10.4.1 Installing Kubernetes for.NET Core Microservices

To run a.NET Core application on Kubernetes, you have to create **Docker images** and define **Kubernetes configuration files**.

1. Create a Docker Image for Each Microservice

    You are using the Dockerfile from Section 10.2.1 to build images of each service.

2. Define Kubernetes Deployment and Service Files

    Create a file called **deployment.yaml to** define a deployment for your service, as shown here:

    ```yaml
    apiVersion: apps/v1
    kind: Deployment
    metadata:
      name: webapi-deployment
    spec:
      replicas: 3
      selector:
        matchLabels:
          app: webapi
      template:
        metadata:
          labels:
            app: webapi
        spec:
          containers:
          - name: webapi
            image: mycloudapp
            ports:
            - containerPort: 80
    ```

Create a **service.yaml** file to define the service that exposes your application:

```
apiVersion: v1
kind: Service
metadata:
  name: webapi-service
spec:
  type: LoadBalancer
  selector:
    app: webapi
  ports:
  - protocol: TCP
    port: 80
    targetPort: 80
```

Deploy to **Kubernetes**

Apply the configurations to your Kubernetes cluster:

```
kubectl apply -f deployment.yaml
kubectl apply -f service.yaml
```

Kubernetes will deploy the application and expose it on a public IP in case you are utilizing cloud provider such as AKS.

10.4.2 Using Helm for Kubernetes Deployments

Helm is an application package manager that aids in deploying hard applications and makes it easier for its users.

1. Create a Helm Chart

```
helm create myapp
```

This will generate a chart with templates to assist you in the process of deploying your application.

2. Tweak the Values and Deploy

Adjust the values within values.yaml to set up how you wish your deployments to be established, then deploy using the command below

```
helm install myapp ./myapp
```

Helm makes it extremely simple to version and distribute complex configurations across multiple environments.

10.5 Serverless Computing with Azure Functions

Microsoft Azure Functions is a serverless compute service that enables you to run functions in response to events. Serverless functions are better suited for developing event-driven architectures or automation without provisioning a server.

10.5.1 Creating an Azure Function with.NET Core

1. Creating a New Azure Functions Project

   ```
   dotnet new func -n MyFunctionApp
   cd MyFunctionApp
   ```

2. Adding a Function

In the solution, add a new function that handles HTTP requests by implementing the following:

```
using Microsoft.AspNetCore.Mvc;
using Microsoft.Azure.WebJobs;
using Microsoft.Azure.WebJobs.Extensions.Http;
using Microsoft.AspNetCore.Http;
using System.Threading.Tasks;

public static class MyFunction
{
    [FunctionName("HelloFunction")]
    public static async Task<IActionResult> Run(
        [HttpTrigger(AuthorizationLevel.Function, "get", "post", Route = null)]
    HttpRequest req)
    {
```

```
        string name = req.Query["name"];
        return new OkObjectResult($"Hello, {name}");
    }
}
```

This function returns a message if accessed via HTTP, replying with "Hello, [name]" based on a query parameter.

3. Running the Function Locally

Run the function with:

```
func start
```

Test it at **http://localhost:7071/api/HelloFunction?name=Azure**.

4. Deploying to Azure

Login to Azure and deploy the function:

```
az login
func azure functionapp publish MyFunctionAppName
```

The function will be available on Azure, automatically scaling with demand.

10.6 Monitoring and Observability with Azure Application Insights

Monitoring is quite important in cloud-native apps, especially for identifying problems in understanding user behavior and hence for performance optimization. With this, Azure Application Insights is a monitoring service and it provides telemetry data related to request rates, responses, and errors.

10.6.1 Including Application Insights in a.NET Core

1. Implement the Application Insights SDK.

   dotnet add package Microsoft.ApplicationInsights.AspNetCore

2. Adding Application Insights in Program.cs

   builder.Services.AddApplicationInsightsTelemetry("Your_InstrumentationKey");

3. Custom Logging Events

```
private readonly TelemetryClient _telemetryClient;

public MyController(TelemetryClient telemetryClient)
{
    _telemetryClient = telemetryClient;
}

public IActionResult Index()
{
    _telemetryClient.TrackEvent("Index Page Loaded");
    return View();
}
```

Use TelemetryClient to log the custom events.

Application Insights will automatically track requests, dependencies, and exceptions, and you can monitor metrics in the **Azure Portal**.

10.7 Best Practices for Cloud-Native Development in.NET Core

1. **Design for Resilience:** Utilize retries and circuit breakers to handle transient errors.

2. **Asynchronous Programming:** Asynchronous methods promote resource utilization and efficiency for cloud applications.

3. **Use Secrets Management:** Secret storage in services such as Azure Key Vault

4. **Containerize Your Application:** This ensures consistent deployments across different environments. Use Docker.

5. **Automate Deployment Pipelines:** These are CI/CD pipelines that automate builds, test, and deployment

10.8 Conclusion

Cloud-native development using the.NET Core 8 is provided so that you can create applications which are scalable and fault tolerant and can work based on the environment where cloud native applications work best. We have learned the steps involved in deploying the applications on **Azure** and **Kubernetes** environments. We also learn **Docker container,** implementation of Azure functions, and Application Insight in monitoring applications. Building upon these patterns and best practices, you can produce scalable, **dynamic cloud readiness application**.

The next chapter has been titled Securing .NET Core 8 Applications, outlining authentication, authorization, encryption, and best practices for securing cloud-native applications.

11. Securing.NET Core 8 Applications

Application security is one of the most important factors while developing trusted applications in these times, as all the applications are interconnected in the cloud.NET Core 8 provides you with many tools and best practices to ensure developers secure their applications. This chapter focuses on authentication, authorization, data encryption, and securing configurations. We also discuss external identity provider integration, JWT, and role-based access control.

11.1 Introduction to.NET Core Security

The data of the application should be protected from unauthorized access; therefore, security in.NET Core will play a role in implementing safety mechanisms in an application that will prevent access and information exposure. Some of the basic elements of securing a.NET Core application are given below:

1. **Authentication:** verifies the identity of the user.

2. **Authorization:** controlling who can access what resource using roles or permissions.

3. **Data Encryption:** protection of data at rest and during transport.

4. **Configuration Management:** safety of sensitive configuration data including connection strings and API keys.

11.2 Authentication in.NET Core with ASP.NET Identity

ASP.NET Identity is a membership system for managing user authentication, including registration, login, and user profile management. ASP.NET Identity integrates with **OAuth2, OpenID Connect,** and external identity providers like Google, Facebook, and Microsoft.

11.2.1 Setup ASP.NET Identity

1. Setup ASP.NET Identity

To set up a new ASP.NET Core Web App that includes Identity support, do the following:

```
dotnet new webapp -n MySecureApp --auth Individual
```

2. Configure Identity at Startup

For those, who want to add the Identity to a project created, install the ASP.NET Core Identity package

```
dotnet add package Microsoft.AspNetCore.Identity.EntityFrameworkCore
```

Configure Identity within Program.cs

```
builder.Services.AddDbContext<ApplicationDbContext>(options =>
    options.UseSqlServer("YourConnectionString"));

builder.Services.AddDefaultIdentity<IdentityUser>(options          =>
options.SignIn.RequireConfirmedAccount = true)
    .AddEntityFrameworkStores<ApplicationDbContext>();

var app = builder.Build();
app.UseAuthentication();
app.UseAuthorization();
```

3. Create Database

Daca you followed everything so far and made everything right, this part would be pretty easy to write.

You can execute all of the commands you see below as demonstrated:

```
dotnet ef migrations add InitialCreate
dotnet ef database update
```

11.2.2 Registration and Login

Once Identity is configured, the template will have register and login pages:

1. **Register Page:** Enables a user to create an account with a username and password.
2. **Login Page:** Allows a registered user to authenticate.

You can override these pages in the **Areas/Identity/Pages/Account** folder.

11.2.3 External Login Providers

ASP.NET Identity supports external login providers such as Google and Facebook. For example, to include Google authentication:

1. **Install Google Authentication Package**

   dotnet add package Microsoft.AspNetCore.Authentication.Google

2. **Set Up Google Authentication**

   In Program.cs, add the following:

   ```
   builder.Services.AddAuthentication().AddGoogle(options =>
   {
     options.ClientId = "YourGoogleClientId";
     options.ClientSecret = "YourGoogleClientSecret";
   });
   ```

3. **Run Application**

Users can now be given the ability to use Google to sign in with this added convenience and security.

11.3 Implementing JWT for Token-Based Authentication

JSON Web Tokens is a compact, secure method of transmitting information between a client and server, maintaining statelessness. JSON Web Tokens are especially ideal for APIs.

11.3.1 JWT Authentication Configuration

Step 1: JWT Auth Configuration

To do this configuration, follow the following step:

1. **Install the JWT Auth Package**

   ```
   dotnet add package Microsoft.AspNetCore.Authentication.JwtBearer
   ```

2. **Configure JWT in Program.cs**

In Program.cs add the JWT authentication scheme

```
var key = Encoding.ASCII.GetBytes("YourSecretKeyHere");

builder.Services.AddAuthentication(options =>
{
    options.DefaultAuthenticateScheme = JwtBearerDefaults.AuthenticationScheme;
    options.DefaultChallengeScheme = JwtBearerDefaults.AuthenticationScheme;
})
.AddJwtBearer(options =>
{
    options.TokenValidationParameters = new TokenValidationParameters
    {
        ValidateIssuerSigningKey = true,
        IssuerSigningKey = new SymmetricSecurityKey(key),
        ValidateIssuer = false,
        ValidateAudience = false
    };
});

var app = builder.Build();
app.UseAuthentication();
app.UseAuthorization();
```

3. Generating JWT Tokens

Create a helper method to generate JWT tokens:

```
public string GenerateJwtToken(string userId)
{
    var tokenHandler = new JwtSecurityTokenHandler();
    var key = Encoding.ASCII.GetBytes("YourSecretKeyHere");

    var tokenDescriptor = new SecurityTokenDescriptor
    {
        Subject = new ClaimsIdentity(new Claim[] { new
Claim(ClaimTypes.NameIdentifier, userId) }),
        Expires = DateTime.UtcNow.AddHours(1),
        SigningCredentials = new SigningCredentials(new SymmetricSecurityKey(key),
SecurityAlgorithms.HmacSha256Signature)
    };

    var token = tokenHandler.CreateToken(tokenDescriptor);
    return tokenHandler.WriteToken(token);
}
```

4. Using the Token in API Requests

To authenticate requests, clients need to send the JWT in the Authorization header:

```
Authorization: Bearer <your-jwt-token>
```

11.4 Authorization with Policies and Role-Based Access Control

Authorization is what you can do once authenticated. There are two ways to have authorization in ASP.NET Core: policies and roles.

11.4.1 Role-Based Authorization

1. Defining Roles

Roles can be set during user creation or edition

```
await userManager.AddToRoleAsync(user, "Admin");
```

2. Controller Actions

Use the attribute [Authorize(Roles = "Admin")] to restrict to those roles

```
[Authorize(Roles = "Admin")]
public IActionResult AdminOnly()
{
    return View();
}
```

Only the users with the Admin role will be able to reach this endpoint.

11.4.2 Policy-Based Authorization

Policies allow for a more fluid mechanism of authorization. In order to use a policy:

1. Define a Policy in Program.cs

```
builder.Services.AddAuthorization(options =>
{
    options.AddPolicy("Over18Only", policy => policy.RequireClaim("Age", "18"));
});
```

2. Apply the Policy

Use the [Authorize(Policy = "Over18Only")] attribute on your controllers or actions:

```
[Authorize(Policy = "Over18Only")]
public IActionResult RestrictedContent()
{
    return View();
}
```

Policies let you enforce quite complex authorization requirements beyond just roles.

11.5 Data Protection and Encryption

Encrypting sensitive data, such as passwords for users, connection strings, and personal information is very important.

11.5.1 Encrypting Sensitive Data with Data Protection API

In terms of help, the data protector for.NET Core serves an important role for this particular purpose: by being there to encrypt as well as decrypt data, DPAPI helps protect sensitive information inside application code.

1. Configuring Data Protection

Within the scope of Program.cs:

```
builder.Services.AddDataProtection();
```

2. Encrypting and Decrypting Data

```
public class EncryptionService
{
    private readonly IDataProtector _protector;

    public EncryptionService(IDataProtectionProvider provider)
    {
        _protector = provider.CreateProtector("MyPurpose");
    }

    public string EncryptData(string data)
    {
        return _protector.Protect(data);
    }

    public string DecryptData(string encryptedData)
    {
        return _protector.Unprotect(encryptedData);
    }
}
```

Data encrypted with DPAPI can only be decrypted by the same application, providing security for sensitive data.

11.5.2 Using Azure Key Vault to Secure Connection Strings and Secrets

Azure Key Vault is a secure way of storing application secrets.

1. **Store Secrets in Azure Key Vault**

Open **Azure Key Vault** and add a new secret.

2. **Add Azure Key Vault to.NET Core**

Install the **Azure.Extensions.AspNetCore.Configuration**.Secrets package:

```
dotnet add package Azure.Extensions.AspNetCore.Configuration.Secrets
```

Add **Key Vault** to your configuration in Program.cs:

```
builder.Configuration.AddAzureKeyVault(
    new Uri("https://<YourVaultName>.vault.azure.net/"),
    new DefaultAzureCredential());
```

The application will safely retrieve secrets from Azure Key Vault and will therefore have protected sensitive information.

11.6 Safe API Endpoints

When developing your APIs, ensure all the endpoints are safe to prevent unauthorized access and leakage of information.

11.6.1 Safe Endpoints with CORS

CORS or Cross-Origin Resource Sharing is a safety feature that denies resources of the web page to be accessed from another origin.

1. **Setup CORS in Program.cs**

```
builder.Services.AddCors(options =>
{
    options.AddPolicy("AllowSpecificOrigin", policy =>
        policy.WithOrigins("https://trusteddomain.com")
            .AllowAnyMethod()
            .AllowAnyHeader());
});

var app = builder.Build();
app.UseCors("AllowSpecificOrigin");
```

2. **Apply CORS Policy to Endpoints**

You can apply the CORS policy globally or on specific endpoints to control access.

11.6.2 Rate Limiting for APIs

Rate limiting limits the number of requests a user makes within a certain time frame to prevent abuse of APIs. It can be implemented using middleware or an external service, such as Azure API Management.

Simple Example: Implementing a Middleware for Simple Rate Limiting

```
public class RateLimitingMiddleware
{
    private static readonly Dictionary<string, DateTime> _clients = new();

    public async Task InvokeAsync(HttpContext context)
    {
        var clientIp = context.Connection.RemoteIpAddress?.ToString();
```

```
        if (_clients.ContainsKey(clientIp) && _clients[clientIp] > DateTime.UtcNow)
        {
            context.Response.StatusCode = StatusCodes.Status429TooManyRequests;
            return;
        }

        _clients[clientIp] = DateTime.UtcNow.AddSeconds(1); // Allow 1 request per
second
        await _next(context);
    }
}
```

Add the middleware in Program.cs to protect endpoints from excessive requests.

11.7 Security Best Practices for.NET Core Applications

1. **Use HTTPS:** Always use HTTPS to encrypt data in transit.

2. **Implement Strong Authentication:** Use OAuth2, OpenID Connect, or JWT for token-based authentication.

3. **Use Parameterized Queries:** Avoid SQL injection by using the ORM libraries like Entity Framework Core or parameterized SQL queries.

4. **Log Security Events**: Log authentication and authorization events with logging libraries.

5. **Minimize Data Exposure:** Do not return sensitive data in the API response.

11.8 Conclusion

Security is the core of any modern application, and.NET Core 8 provides rich tools for secure authentication, authorization, encryption, and configuration management. This chapter covered **ASP.NET Identity** for user management, **JWT** for API authentication, policy-based authorization, and data encryption with **Data Protection API** and **Azure Key Vault.** All these techniques and best practices will help you build resilient applications that protect user data and prevent unauthorized access.

We'll dive into **Blazor and Full-stack Development in.NET Core 8** in the next chapter. There we explore how to build interactive, client-side web applications with C# and Blazor and, hence, make modern web experiences possible without resorting to JavaScript.

12. Blazor Full Stack in.NET Core 8

Blazor lets developers build interactive web apps with **C#** and. **NET** instead of JavaScript. Developers can build client-side applications entirely with C#, and their technology stack is the same both for front-end code and back-end code. That way, you can craft rich, modern web apps using components, real-time interactivity, and great integration with.NET Core 8.

This chapter covers the basics of Blazor, including the two main models of **Blazor Server** and **Blazor WebAssembly**, building reusable components, managing state, and integrating with REST APIs to create a full-stack.NET Core 8 application.

12.1 Overview of Blazor: Server vs. WebAssembly

Blazor provides two main hosting models:

1. **Blazor Server:** It runs on the server and communicates with the client via a SignalR connection. This model is very fast to load and ideal for applications that need real-time data updates. However, it does depend on a constant server connection.

2. **Blazor WebAssembly:** This model runs completely in the browser using WebAssembly and has no dependency on the server side. This model is ideal for offline and fully client-side applications but has a larger initial load time compared to Blazor Server.

Model Selection: Use Blazor Server when you need immediate interactive response from the server; use Blazor WebAssembly when your application is extremely client-based and requires off-line capabilities.

12.2 Creating a Blazor Project

Both Blazor Server and Blazor WebAssembly projects can be created by using either the **.NET CLI** or **Visual Studio**.

12.2.1 Creating a Blazor Server Project

To create a new Blazor Server application, run the following:

```
dotnet new blazorserver -n BlazorServerApp
```

12.2.2 Creating a Blazor WebAssembly Project

Run the following command to create a new Blazor WebAssembly app:

```
dotnet new blazorwasm -n BlazorWasmApp
```

Go into the project directory and run the application:

```
cd BlazorWasmApp
dotnet run
```

Head to **http://localhost:5000** to see your Blazor application in action.

12.3 Understanding Blazor Components

A Blazor application is constructed of components. A component is the reusable UI building block with its **markup (HTML)** and **the code (C#) associated** with it as being implemented in **C#**. The same thing in Blazor but can be applied throughout an application - a Blazor counterpart of the Razor pages is called component.

12.3.1 Simple Component Creation

For a Blazor, its component is by having an extension in **.razor**. So you make the **CounterComponent.razor**.

```
<h3>Counter</h3>
<p>Current count: @count</p>
<button @onclick="IncrementCount">Click me</button>

@code {
  private int count = 0;

  private void IncrementCount()
  {
    count++;
  }
}
```

This is a component showing a counter and an increment button. The **@onclick** directive binds the button's click event to the **IncrementCount** method.

12.3.2 Using the Component in Other Pages

To use the **CounterComponent** in a page, you simply reference it in another component or page:

Index.razor:

```
@page "/"
<h1>Welcome to the Counter Page</h1>

<CounterComponent />
```

Blazor knows **CounterComponent** is a component and puts it inside the Index page.

12.4 Working with Parameters and Events

Blazor components can have **parameters** and **raise** events in order to communicate with other components.

12.4.1 Passing Parameters

We will update the **CounterComponent** to accept an initial count as a parameter:

CounterComponent.razor

```
<h3>Counter</h3>
<p>Current count: @count</p>
<button @onclick="IncrementCount">Click me</button>

@code {
  [Parameter]
  public int InitialCount { get; set; }

  private int count;

  protected override void OnInitialized()
  {
    count = InitialCount;
  }

  private void IncrementCount()
  {
    count++;
  }
}
```

The **[Parameter]** attribute is used to make **InitialCount** a parameter.

The **OnInitialized** method establishes the default count when the component initializes.

You can pass a parameter in the calling page using property syntax:

Index.razor :

```
<CounterComponent InitialCount="10" />
```

The counter will start counting from 10 instead of 0.

12.4.2 Raising Events

There are times we want the parent component to be notified when an event is raised by the child. We will use **EventCallback** for that.

CounterComponent.razor :

```razor
<h3>Counter</h3>
<p>Current count: @count</p>
<button @onclick="IncrementCount">Click me</button>

@code {
  private int count = 0;

  [Parameter]
  public EventCallback<int> OnCountChanged { get; set; }

  private async Task IncrementCount()
  {
    count++;
    await OnCountChanged.InvokeAsync(count);
  }
}
```

In the parent component, bind to the **OnCountChanged** callback to handle the event:

Index.razor:

```razor
<CounterComponent OnCountChanged="HandleCountChanged" />

<p>Current count from CounterComponent: @currentCount</p>

@code {
  private int currentCount = 0;

  private void HandleCountChanged(int newCount)
  {
    currentCount = newCount;
  }
}
```

12.5 Managing Application State

Blazor provides multiple ways to manage application state across components, including **dependency injection, state containers,** and **session storage** for Blazor WebAssembly.

12.5.1 Dependency Injection as a Means to Handle State

We could define a state service and then inject it into many other components.

1. Implementing A State Service: We then create a service named as AppState.cs for storing our shared data.

AppState.cs

```csharp
public class AppState
{
    public int SharedCounter { get; private set; }

    public void IncrementCounter()
    {
        SharedCounter++;
    }
}
```

2. **Register the Service:** Register AppState as a singleton in Program.cs.

```csharp
builder.Services.AddSingleton<AppState>();
```

3. Inject the Service in Components: Use dependency injection to inject AppState in your components.

CounterComponent.razor:

```csharp
@inject AppState appState
```

```
<h3>Shared Counter</h3>
<p>Counter value: @appState.SharedCounter</p>
<button @onclick="appState.IncrementCounter">Increment</button>
```

Using **AppState** as a singleton, the counter value is shared among all the components that inject this service.

12.6 Calling REST APIs in Blazor

Blazor applications often interact with a REST API when reading and writing data. There's an **HttpClient** class in Blazor that makes Http requests.

12.6.1 Setting up HttpClient in Blazor

HttpClient is already enabled within Blazor WebAssembly, but in Blazor Server you have to register HttpClient through the dependency injection system like the following line:

```
builder.Services.AddHttpClient();
```

12.6.2 Making an API

In this chapter we implement a **ProductService:** a service which reads the products from a REST API.

ProductService.cs

```
using System.Net.Http;
using System.Net.Http.Json;
using System.Threading.Tasks;

public class ProductService
{
    private readonly HttpClient _httpClient;

    public ProductService(HttpClient httpClient)
    {
        _httpClient = httpClient;
    }
```

```csharp
    public async Task<List<Product>> GetProductsAsync()
    {
        return
await
_httpClient.GetFromJsonAsync<List<Product>>("https://api.example.com/produc
ts");
    }
}
```

Register **ProductService** in **Program.cs**:

```csharp
builder.Services.AddScoped<ProductService>();
```

Inject and use ProductService in a component:

ProductList.razor:

```razor
@page "/products"
@inject ProductService ProductService

<h3>Product List</h3>
@if (products == null)
{
    <p>Loading...</p>
}
else
{
    <ul>
        @foreach (var product in products)
        {
            <li>@product.Name - @product.Price</li>
        }
    </ul>
}

@code {
    private List<Product> products;

    protected override async Task OnInitializedAsync()
    {
```

```
        products = await ProductService.GetProductsAsync();
    }
}
```

12.7 Building Real-Time Applications with SignalR

Blazor Server applications support **SignalR** for real-time communication. SignalR allows the server to send real-time updates to the client, such as in chat applications, notification, and live feeds.

12.7.1. Setting Up SignalR

Add SignalR Hub: Define a SignalR hub to handle real-time communications.

1. **ChatHub.cs**

```
using Microsoft.AspNetCore.SignalR;

public class ChatHub : Hub
{
    public async Task SendMessage(string user, string message)
    {
        await Clients.All.SendAsync("ReceiveMessage", user, message);
    }
}
```

2. **Configure SignalR in Program.cs:**

```
var app = builder.Build();
app.MapHub<ChatHub>("/chathub");
```

3. **Create a Chat Component in Blazor:**

ChatComponent.razor:

```razor
@inject NavigationManager Navigation
@implements IAsyncDisposable

<h3>Chat</h3>
<input @bind="user" placeholder="Enter your name" />
<input @bind="message" placeholder="Enter message" />
<button @onclick="SendMessage">Send</button>
<ul>
    @foreach (var msg in messages)
    {
        <li>@msg</li>
    }
</ul>

@code {
    private HubConnection? hubConnection;
    private List<string> messages = new();
    private string user;
    private string message;

    protected override async Task OnInitializedAsync()
    {
        hubConnection = new HubConnectionBuilder()
            .WithUrl(Navigation.ToAbsoluteUri("/chathub"))
            .Build();

        hubConnection.On<string, string>("ReceiveMessage", (user, message) =>
        {
            messages.Add($"{user}: {message}");
            InvokeAsync(StateHasChanged);
        });

        await hubConnection.StartAsync();
    }

    private async Task SendMessage()
    {
        if (hubConnection is not null)
        {
            await hubConnection.SendAsync("SendMessage", user, message);
        }
    }
}
```

```
public async ValueTask DisposeAsync()
{
    if (hubConnection is not null)
    {
        await hubConnection.DisposeAsync();
    }
}
}
```

It uses a connection to the ChatHub for sending and receiving messages in real time.

12.8 Best Practices in Developing Blazor

1. **Apply Components for Reusability:** Decompose the UI into reusable components.

2. **Optimize Performance:** Use minimum network calls and perform operations in asynchronous fashion.

3. **Be careful about the State:** Implement shared state using dependency injection.

4. **Keep Sensitive Data Safe:** Do not keep sensitive data in the local Blazor WebAssembly. Client may get access to this.

In this chapter, we'll explore Blazor-a very powerful framework for creating interactive web applications using C# on the server and client sides. We walked through creating and using components, handling parameters and events, managing application state, making calls to REST APIs, and integration with real-time updates from SignalR. These enable full-stack development using.NET Core 8, thus allowing developers to build modern, robust applications without depending extensively on JavaScript.

The next chapter would be on Interoperability and Cross-Platform Development with.NET Core. This includes integration of the.NET application with JavaScript, working with native APIs, and cross-platform application development.

13. Interoperability and Cross-Platform Development in .NET Core 8

With the increasing diversity of platforms, devices, and operating systems, cross-platform development has become essential. **.NET Core 8** enables developers to build applications that run on various platforms, including Windows, macOS, and Linux. Additionally, **interoperability** features allow .NET applications to communicate with other languages, APIs, and platforms, making it possible to integrate .NET code with JavaScript, native APIs, and cross-platform tools.

This chapter will guide you through key topics in cross-platform development with .NET Core 8, including working with **JavaScript interop** in Blazor, **P/Invoke** for native API calls, creating cross-platform applications with **MAUI (Multi-platform App UI),** and developing **CLI** tools.

13.1 Understanding Cross-Platform Support in .NET Core 8

.NET Core is a fully cross-platform framework, meaning applications built on .NET Core 8 can run on:

- **Windows:** Compatible with Windows APIs, libraries, and services.

- **macOS:** Can be executed natively on macOS with support for Apple's ecosystem.

- **Linux:** Provides high-performance runtime support on various Linux distributions, ideal for server and cloud environments.

.NET Core's compatibility with multiple platforms comes from its runtime and Base Class Library (BCL), which offers OS-specific implementations and unified APIs for platform-agnostic development.

13.2 Working with JavaScript Interoperability in Blazor

Blazor provides **JavaScript Interop** to allow .NET code to interact with Java
Script functions and vice versa. This is particularly useful for accessing browser-specific APIs
or leveraging JavaScript libraries in Blazor applications.

13.2.1 Invoking JavaScript Functions from C#

In Blazor, you can call JavaScript functions from C# code using the **IJSRuntime** service.

Example: Calling a JavaScript Function from C#

1. Define the JavaScript function in **wwwroot/js/interop.js**:

   ```javascript
   function showAlert(message) {
      alert(message);
   }
   ```

2. Register the JavaScript file in **_Layout.cshtml** or **index.html**:

   ```html
   <script src="js/interop.js"></script>
   ```

3. **Invoke the JavaScript function** in a Blazor component:

   ```razor
   @inject IJSRuntime JS

   <button @onclick="ShowAlert">Show Alert</button>

   @code {
      private async Task ShowAlert()
      {
         await JS.InvokeVoidAsync("showAlert", "Hello from C#");
      }
   }
   ```

Here, **InvokeVoidAsync** calls the **showAlert** JavaScript function with the message
parameter.

13.2.2 Calling C# Methods from JavaScript

You can also call C# methods from JavaScript by using **DotNetObjectReference**.

1. **Define the C# method in a Blazor component:**

```
@code {
  [JSInvokable]
  public static void ShowMessageFromJavaScript(string message)
  {
    Console.WriteLine($"Message from JavaScript: {message}");
  }
}
```

2. **Invoke the C# method from JavaScript:**

```
DotNet.invokeMethodAsync('YourAssemblyName', 'ShowMessageFromJavaScript',
'Hello from JavaScript');
```

This setup allows two-way communication between JavaScript and Blazor, enabling greater flexibility in handling complex UI interactions.

13.3 Calling Native APIs with P/Invoke

Platform Invocation (P/Invoke) enables .NET Core applications to call native C or C++ libraries. This is especially useful for integrating OS-level functionality or leveraging existing native code.

13.3.1 Understanding P/Invoke

P/Invoke allows you to declare functions from a native library using the **DllImport** attribute and then call them as if they were normal .NET methods.

13.3.2 Example: Calling a Native Library

Let's say you want to use the **MessageBox** function from the Windows API.

1. **Declare the function in C#:**

```
using System.Runtime.InteropServices;

public class NativeMethods
{
    [DllImport("user32.dll", CharSet = CharSet.Unicode)]
    public static extern int MessageBox(IntPtr hWnd, string text, string caption, uint type);
}
```

2. **Call the function:**

```
NativeMethods.MessageBox(IntPtr.Zero, "Hello, World!", "MessageBox from P/Invoke", 0);
```

This code will show a native Windows message box.

Note: P/Invoke works on Windows but can also be adapted to call native libraries on macOS and Linux. However, be mindful of library compatibility across operating systems.

13.4 Cross-Platform Desktop Applications with .NET MAUI

.NET Multi-platform App UI (MAUI) is a framework for building cross-platform desktop and mobile applications using a single codebase. With .NET MAUI, you can create applications for Windows, macOS, iOS, and Android.

13.4.1 Setting Up a .NET MAUI Project

To get started with .NET MAUI, ensure that you have the .NET MAUI workload installed.

1. **Install the .NET MAUI workload (if not already installed):**

   ```
   dotnet workload install maui
   ```

2. **Create a new MAUI project:**

   ```
   dotnet new maui -n MyMauiApp
   ```

3. **Run the project:**

   ```
   dotnet build MyMauiApp -t:Run -f net8.0-android # For Android
   dotnet build MyMauiApp -t:Run -f net8.0-ios     # For iOS
   dotnet build MyMauiApp -t:Run -f net8.0-windows # For Windows
   ```

13.4.2 Building a Simple UI in .NET MAUI

MAUI uses **XAML** for UI definitions, similar to WPF or Xamarin.Forms.

MainPage.xaml:

```xml
<ContentPage xmlns="http://schemas.microsoft.com/dotnet/2021/maui"
      xmlns:x="http://schemas.microsoft.com/winfx/2009/xaml"
      x:Class="MyMauiApp.MainPage">
  <VerticalStackLayout>
    <Label Text="Welcome to .NET MAUI!"
        FontSize="32"
        HorizontalOptions="Center" />
    <Button Text="Click Me" Clicked="OnButtonClicked" />
    <Label x:Name="CounterLabel" Text="0" FontSize="24"
HorizontalOptions="Center" />
  </VerticalStackLayout>
</ContentPage>
```

MainPage.xaml.cs:

```csharp
public partial class MainPage : ContentPage
{
    private int count = 0;
```

```csharp
public MainPage()
{
    InitializeComponent();
}

private void OnButtonClicked(object sender, EventArgs e)
{
    count++;
    CounterLabel.Text = $"Count: {count}";
}
}
```

This simple UI has a button and a label. Each time the button is clicked, the counter is incremented.

13.4.3 Platform-Specific Code in .NET MAUI

MAUI allows you to write platform-specific code using dependency injection or compiler directives.

Example: Platform-Specific Code for Android:

```csharp
#if ANDROID
    // Android-specific code
#endif
```

By using these techniques, you can write applications that leverage native functionality on each platform.

13.5 Developing Command-Line Applications

.NET Core 8 makes it easy to develop cross-platform command-line applications that can be run on any operating system.

13.5.1 Creating a CLI Application

Use the following command to create a new console application:

```
dotnet new console -n MyCliApp
```

Program.cs:

```csharp
using System;

class Program
{
    static void Main(string[] args)
    {
        Console.WriteLine("Welcome to My CLI App!");

        if (args.Length > 0)
        {
            Console.WriteLine($"You provided {args.Length} arguments:");
            foreach (var arg in args)
            {
                Console.WriteLine(arg);
            }
        }
        else
        {
            Console.WriteLine("No arguments provided.");
        }
    }
}
```

To run this CLI application with arguments, use:

```
dotnet run -- arg1 arg2 arg3
```

13.5.2 Adding Command-Line Parsing with System.CommandLine

The System.CommandLine package simplifies parsing complex command-line arguments.

1. **Install System.CommandLine:**

```
dotnet add package System.CommandLine
```

2. Use CommandLineBuilder to Define Commands:

```
using System.CommandLine;
using System.CommandLine.Invocation;

var rootCommand = new RootCommand
{
    new Option<string>("--name", "Your name"),
    new Option<int>("--age", "Your age")
};

rootCommand.Description = "My CLI Application";

rootCommand.Handler = CommandHandler.Create<string, int>((name, age) =>
{
    Console.WriteLine($"Hello, {name}. You are {age} years old.");
});

return await rootCommand.InvokeAsync(args);
```

Run the application with:

```
dotnet run -- --name John --age 30
```

This approach makes it easy to build flexible, robust command-line applications with structured argument parsing.

13.6 Integrating .NET Core with Python and Other Languages

.NET Core provides a runtime interoperability feature through .NET for Apache Spark and the Python.NET library, enabling integration with other languages like Python.

13.6.1 Using Python.NET for .NET and Python Interop

Python.NET allows you to call Python code from .NET and vice versa.

1. **Install Python.NET:**

   dotnet add package Python.Runtime

2. **Writing C# Code to Call Python Scripts:**

   ```csharp
   using Python.Runtime;

   public class PythonInterop
   {
     public void CallPythonCode()
     {
       using (Py.GIL())
       {
         dynamic np = Py.Import("numpy");
         dynamic result = np.array(new int[] { 1, 2, 3 }) * 2;
         Console.WriteLine(result);
       }
     }
   }
   ```

In this example, C# code interacts with Python's **NumPy** library to perform array operations.

13.6.2 Cross-Language Machine Learning with ML.NET and Python

With ML.NET and Python.NET, you can build machine learning pipelines in .NET Core using models created in Python.

Example:

1. Train a model in Python using TensorFlow or PyTorch.

2. Export the model in **ONNX** format.

3. Load and use the model in a .NET Core application with **ML.NET's** ONNX support.

This integration allows you to combine Python's machine learning libraries with .NET Core applications, enabling advanced data analytics and AI-driven features.

13.7 Best Practices for Cross-Platform Development

1. **Use Platform-Agnostic Code:** Avoid OS-specific code unless necessary.

2. **Write Portable Libraries:** Design your .NET libraries to be usable on all target platforms.

3. **Optimize for Performance on Each Platform:** Test on each platform to ensure consistency and performance.

4. **Use Dependency Injection for Interoperability:** Structure code to support dependency injection for platform-specific services.

5. **Leverage Cross-Platform Tools: Use** .NET MAUI, Blazor, and command-line tools to maximize reach.

13.8 Conclusion

In this chapter, we explored the cross-platform and interoperability capabilities of **.NET Core 8**. We covered using JavaScript interop in Blazor applications, working with P/Invoke for native code calls, building cross-platform desktop and mobile applications with **.NET MAUI,** developing **CLI** tools with .NET Core, and integrating with Python for data science and machine learning. With these tools and best practices, .NET Core 8 allows developers to build versatile applications that work seamlessly across diverse environments and platforms.

In the next chapter, we'll delve into **Performance Optimization** and **Best Practices** in .NET Core 8, focusing on strategies for improving application speed, reducing memory usage, and enhancing overall efficiency.

14. Performance Optimization and Best Practices in NET Core 8

Building responsive, efficient, and scalable applications requires optimization of performance. Several features and improvements in .NET Core 8 make it easier to build high-performance applications. This chapter explores key techniques for improving performance: memory management, asynchronous programming, optimizing LINQ queries, caching usage, and best practices for profiling and benchmarking .NET applications.

14.1 Optimizing Memory Usage

Efficient memory management is the need of the application, mainly in cloud and large scale applications. DotNet Core has a garbage collector (GC) that automatically reclaims memory, but it's always good to have some idea regarding how memory is being allocated and deallocated so that you can make some optimizations.

14.1.1 Using Structs for Lightweight Data

A struct is a value type stored on the stack making it more efficient to small, frequently used objects. Use structs for small, immutable data structures.

Example:

```
public struct Point
{
    public int X { get; }
    public int Y { get; }

    public Point(int x, int y)
    {
        X = x;
        Y = y;
    }
}
```

Use structs only for lightweight data, as large structs could degrade performance due to overhead of the copy.

14.1.2 Minimize Unnecessary Object Instantiations

Many allocations can make garbage collector work very hard, and performance degrades. StringBuilder is designed for string concatenation instead of creating a lot of string objects in the heap.

StringBuilder Instead of String Concatenation

```
var builder = new StringBuilder();
for (int i = 0; i < 1000; i++)
{
    builder.Append("text");
}
string result = builder.ToString();
```

StringBuilder minimizes memory allocations, thus reducing the pressure on the GC.

14.1.3 Avoid Boxing and Unboxing

Boxing occurs when a value type is converted into a reference type while unboxing converts it back. Those conversions are pricey. So try to avoid them, especially in performance-critical sections.

Example : Avoid Boxing with Generics

```
public void ProcessNumbers<T>(T number) where T : struct
{
    // Process number without boxing
}
```

Using where T : struct ensures the number remains a value type, avoiding boxing.

14.2 Improving Asynchronous and Parallel Programming

Asynchronous programming is useful for improving I/O-bound applications, while parallelism is the best option for CPU-bound tasks.

14.2.1 Efficient use of async and await

Using async and await can avoid blocking calls in I/O-bound applications. Tast.Wait() or Result should not be used; they can lead to deadlocks or degraded performance.

Example: Asynchronous Database Call

```
public async Task<List<Data>> GetDataAsync()
{
    using var context = new AppDbContext();
    return await context.Data.ToListAsync();
}
```

Using await in the following code doesn't block the thread but keeps the application running responsive.

14.2.2 Using Task.WhenAll for Parallel Execution

Use Task.WhenAll to run multiple asynchronous tasks in parallel. This comes in handy for tasks that are an ideal candidate for parallel execution.

Example: Executing Multiple Tasks in Parallel

```
public async Task ProcessDataAsync()
{
    var task1 = FetchDataFromApiAsync();
    var task2 = ReadFileAsync("filePath");
```

```
    var task3 = CalculateValuesAsync();

    await Task.WhenAll(task1, task2, task3);
}
```

Using Task.WhenAll, all the tasks are awaited in parallel, shortening total execution time.

14.2.3 Using Parallel.For and PLINQ for CPU-Bound Tasks

Parallel.For and Parallel LINQ (PLINQ) can be used to execute CPU-bound operations in parallel.

Example: Using Parallel.For for a CPU-Bound Operation

```
Parallel.For(0, 1000, i =>
{
    PerformComputation(i);
});
```

The loop can be paralleled which can make an enormous difference in execution time in multi-core processors.

14.3 Optimizing LINQ Queries

LINQ is a significant feature of C#, but no doubt it can be misused to develop bottlenecks in performance.

14.3.1 Using AsEnumerable for In-Memory LINQ Operations

AsEnumerable can prevent unnecessary round trips to the database with Entity Framework Core, now convert the IQueryable result to IEnumerable, forcing its execution in memory.

Example: Filter in Memory

```
var query = context.Products
  .Where(p => p.Category == "Electronics")
  .AsEnumerable()
  .Where(p => p.Price > 100);
```

Only the first query will be executed in the database; filtering is done in memory for the additional result.

14.3.2 Compiled Queries in Entity Framework

Compiled queries in Entity Framework Core allow for performance advantages by reusing the plans.

Compiled Query for Entity Framework

```
public static readonly Func<AppDbContext, int, Product> GetProductById =
    EF.CompileQuery((AppDbContext       context,       int       id)       =>
context.Products.FirstOrDefault(p => p.Id == id));

var product = GetProductById(context, 5);
```

Compiled queries are good because it enhances the execution time of the queries. Because compilation happens only once and then every time it just calls with parameters, it has avoided repetitive query compilation.

14.3.3 N+1 Problem

N+1 problem means for each item, it has to execute the query. For an efficient approach, use Include to load related entities in one go.

Example: How to Overcome N+1 Problem using Include

```
var orders = context.Orders
    .Include(o => o.OrderItems)
    .ToList();
```

Using Include: will prevent direct database calls, thereby reducing latency as well as performance.

14.4 Caching for Performance

Caching is a good strategy to minimize the number of data base or API calls if the data is accessed a lot.

14.4.1 In-Memory Caching in .NET Core

Use MemoryCache to cache data in memory. That's where high read rates and moderate memory usage go hand in hand.

Example: Using MemoryCache

1. **Registering IMemoryCache in Program.cs**

   ```
   builder.Services.AddMemoryCache();
   ```

2. **Applying caching in a service**

   ```
   public class ProductService
   {
       private readonly IMemoryCache _cache;

       public ProductService(IMemoryCache cache)
       {
   ```

```
      _cache = cache;
    }

    public Product GetProduct(int id)
    {
      return _cache.GetOrCreate($"Product_{id}", entry =>
      {
        entry.AbsoluteExpirationRelativeToNow = TimeSpan.FromMinutes(5);
        return FetchProductFromDatabase(id);  // Expensive operation
      });
    }
  }
}
```

Cache in-memory reduces the time to access data by keeping it locally within an application process.

14.4.2 Distributed Caching using Redis

Redis is an in-memory data store that is widely used for developing distributed applications supporting distributed caching across many nodes.

1. **Install Redis Client:**

   dotnet add package Microsoft.Extensions.Caching.StackExchangeRedis

2. **Configure Redis in Program.cs:**

   ```
   builder.Services.AddStackExchangeRedisCache(options =>
   {
     options.Configuration = "localhost:6379";
     options.InstanceName = "SampleInstance";
   });
   ```

3. **Use Redis Cache:**

   ```
   public class ProductService
   {
   ```

```csharp
private readonly IDistributedCache _cache;

public ProductService(IDistributedCache cache)
{
    _cache = cache;
}

public async Task<Product> GetProductAsync(int id)
{
    var cachedProduct = await _cache.GetStringAsync($"Product_{id}");
    if (!string.IsNullOrEmpty(cachedProduct))
    {
        return JsonSerializer.Deserialize<Product>(cachedProduct);
    }

    var product = FetchProductFromDatabase(id);
    await                              _cache.SetStringAsync($"Product_{id}",
JsonSerializer.Serialize(product));
    return product;
}
}
```

Distributed caching with Redis improves performance and scales better across multiple application instances.

14.5 Using Minimal APIs for Lightweight Endpoints

Minimal APIs support a more minimalist approach to declarative HTTP endpoints, meaning they have less overhead compared to traditional ASP.NET Core applications in smaller applications or microservices.

Minimal API in .NET Core

```csharp
var builder = WebApplication.CreateBuilder(args);
var app = builder.Build();

app.MapGet("/api/product/{id}", (int id) =>
```

```
    {
        var product = GetProductById(id);
        return product is not null ? Results.Ok(product) : Results.NotFound();
    });

    app.Run();
```

Minimal APIs have less boilerplate code than any other alternatives, making them a good option for small microservices or applications with few endpoints.

14.6 Native AOT

Native AOT compiles .NET applications directly to native code, thus making the startup performance improve and memory usage better.

1. Enable AOT Compilation:

In your .csproj file, add the following:

```
<PropertyGroup>
    <PublishAot>true</PublishAot>
</PropertyGroup>
```

2. Publish your application:

```
dotnet publish -c Release
```

Native AOT makes your applications start up faster and run faster at runtime. This makes them excellent for CLI tools, microservices, and applications where high performance is a constraint.

14.7 Profiling and Benchmarking .NET Core Applications

Profiling and benchmarking can also be used as two crucial techniques that can lead to the discovery of performance bottlenecks, execution times measurement, and optimization of code. There exist both inbuilt tools and third-party libraries, created under the .NET Core platforms, which can be of great benefit for developers who need to understand the performances of their applications.

14.7.1 Runtime Metrics Using dotnet-counters

Dotnet-counters is a command-line tool for getting real-time performance metrics on CPU usage, memory, garbage collection, and many more. The tool is useful for live applications, especially while testing their applications for performances.

Install and Execute dotnet-counters:

1. **Execute your application:**

    dotnet run

2. **Monitor the Application:**

    In another terminal, execute:

    dotnet-counters monitor -p <process-id>

Replace <process-id> with the ID of your running applicationid; you can get the ID from dotnet-counters ps. This command produces real-time metrics about the CPU usage, GC activity, etc.

14.7.2 Profiling and Debugging with dotnet-trace

dotnet-trace captures precise traces of the execution of a .NET Core application, including perhaps method calls, thread activity, and memory usage.

1. **Run dotnet-trace:**

Run dotnet-trace with your application's process ID:

```
dotnet-trace collect -p <process-id> -o trace.nettrace
```

This will generate a file .nettrace, which will contain detailed trace data.

2. Analyzing the Trace:

Open the .nettrace file in PerfView or Visual Studio for accurate analysis. One can locate methods consuming more CPU, analyze memory-allocation patterns, and pinpoint the bottlenecks.

14.7.3 Benchmarking performance with BenchmarkDotNet

BenchmarkDotNet is the most popular library to benchmark your .NET code. It makes automatic benchmarking via a strategy that isolates the executing code, measures average execution time and gives rich reports.

1. Installation of BenchmarkDotNet

Install BenchmarkDotNet package into your project through the following command in the terminal:

```
dotnet add package BenchmarkDotNet
```

2. Create a Benchmark Class

A benchmark class has to contain benchmark methods. You must annotate each method with the [Benchmark] attribute.

```
using BenchmarkDotNet.Attributes;
using BenchmarkDotNet.Running;

public class SortingBenchmarks
{
    private readonly int[] data = Enumerable.Range(0, 1000).OrderByDescending(x
=> x).ToArray();

    [Benchmark]
```

```csharp
public void ArraySort()
{
    Array.Sort(data);
}

[Benchmark]
public void LinqOrderBy()
{
    var sortedData = data.OrderBy(x => x).ToArray();
}
}
```

3. Run the Benchmark:

Add a Main method to run the benchmarks:

```csharp
public class Program
{
    public static void Main(string[] args)
    {
        BenchmarkRunner.Run<SortingBenchmarks>();
    }
}
```

When you run this application, BenchmarkDotNet will generate a detailed report showing execution times, memory allocations, and a comparison of the benchmarked methods.

BenchmarkDotNet is great for trying optimizations and verifying performance improvements across various implementations.

14.8 Best Practices for I/O and Networking Optimization

I/O and networking operations should be optimized for applications that have intensive data processing, file operations, or networking.

14.8.1 Optimizing File I/O

While performing file I/O, ensure that you specifically pay attention to reducing the time taken to access a disk and consuming as little memory as possible.

1. Use Buffered Streams:

Buffered streams minimize the number of direct calls to disk as they can buffer data in memory.

Example:

```
using var fileStream = new FileStream("largefile.txt", FileMode.Open,
FileAccess.Read);
using var bufferedStream = new BufferedStream(fileStream, bufferSize: 8192);
```

Using BufferedStream with adequate buffer size decreases I/O time significantly with large files.

2. Read and Write Data Asynchronously:

Avoid blocking threads using asynchronous methods for reading and writing. Large files call for avoiding blocked thread for the most part.

Example:

```
using var stream = new FileStream("output.txt", FileMode.Create, FileAccess.Write,
FileShare.None, 4096, true);
await stream.WriteAsync(data, 0, data.Length);
```

Asynchronous I/O operations reduce the time a thread is blocked by an I/O operation.

14.8.2 Optimizing Network Calls

When network operations are involved, this often becomes a hotspot, hence API calls and data transfer have to be optimized for performance.

1. Use HttpClient Responsibility

HttpClient is designed to be reused to make multiple requests. The alternative - making a new instance for each request - will lead to socket exhaustion and slower performance.

EXAMPLE

```
private static readonly HttpClient httpClient = new HttpClient();
```

Reusing a single instance of HttpClient improves connection reuse and general performance.

2. Enabling Gzip Compression

Enable gzip compression of the data transferred over the network. This also reduces the size of data transferred over the network.

Example

```
httpClient.DefaultRequestHeaders.AcceptEncoding.Add(new
System.Net.Http.Headers.StringWithQualityHeaderValue("gzip"));
```

3. Use Asynchronous Networking APIs:

Use await with network requests to improve responsiveness.

Example

```
var response = await httpClient.GetStringAsync("https://api.example.com/data");
```

Asynchronous networking prevents blocking calls on the network from blocking other operations.

14.9 Summary of Performance Best Practices

Here are the good practices for improving performance in .NET Core applications:

1. **Memory Optimization:**

   - Make use of structs so that you can have lightweight accessed data.

   - Avoid unnecessary object allocations; you can make use of StringBuilder when you do any string manipulation

   - Avoid boxing and unboxing in value types

2. **Asynchronous Programming**

   - You can make use of async/await for I/O-bound tasks.

   - You can make use of Task.WhenAll to run multiple tasks.

   - Make use of Parallel.For for CPU-bound operations that can utilize multi-core processors.

3. **LINQ and Database Access**

   - Use AsEnumerable for the filtering operation in memory

   - Use Compiled queries in Entity Framework Core.

- Minimize the N+1 query problem with Includes, eager loading related entities

4. Use caching

- Apply in-memory caching on data that is local and accessed frequently

- Use distributed caching like Redis to provide highly scalable caching across many instances

5. Minimal APIs

- Use Minimal APIs for light-weight microservices or small sets of API endpoints when overhead in an application should be minimized

6. Profiling and Benchmarking

- Use dotnet-counters for runtime metrics

- Use dotnet-trace to have highly detailed traces around your application

- Use BenchmarkDotNet to measure your code executions and compare approaches

7. Native AOT

- Enable AOT compilation to make startup times faster and runtime performance improvements available for CLI tools and microservices.

8. I/O and Networking:

- Use buffered streams for access to large files.

- Use HttpClient in a least-invasive manner by reusing instances

- Enable Gzip compression and use async network requests to reduce blocking

14.10 Real-World Scenario: Optimizing an API-Driven Web Application

To illustrate these optimizations, we will look at an existing high-traffic web application that depends on an enormous, complex API to optimize.

Optimize Database Access:

Problem: The API makes frequent calls for the product details, resulting in an enormous load on the database from queries.

Solution: Keep product-related information in Redis cache instead of calling the database immediately, which reduces the response time.

Optimize Network Calls:

Problems: There are a high number of external API calls made by the application to get the conversion rates for various currencies.

Solution: Cache API responses in memory and set them to expire after 10 minutes. This eliminates redundant network calls and makes the application faster.

Improve Concurrency:

Problem: APIs process in sequence, resulting in huge wait times for requests during peak hours.

Solution: Use Task.WhenAll to process several requests in parallel, which in fact improves through-put.

Shrink Response Size:

Problem: Large payloads for JSON slow down the response time due to limited bandwidth users.

Solution: Compress JSON responses with Gzip and un-necessary properties in the API responses to minimize payload size.

Monitor and Profile Performance:

Problem: CPU usage is high at constant intervals, affecting response times.

Solution: dotnet-counters dotnet-trace Identify the bottlenecks and dissect method calls. Optimize the hotspots-found - viz., the methods that are called frequently.

The application of these optimizations gives a reduction in the response time of the API-driven application. The throughput improves, and server resource consumption drops, leading to greater user benefit and higher returns on investments.

14.11 Conclusion

Performance optimization in .NET Core 8 is obtained through memory management, efficient I/O handling, caching, and concurrent programming. When developers follow best practices using .NET Core profiling and benchmarking tools, that is assured to the developers about their applications being fast, responsive, and scalable. In this chapter, we covered some of the essentials around memory usage improvement, asynchronous programming, LINQ optimization, and network and I/O operations. Let's also look at a few real-world scenarios and tools in order to diagnose and solve performance problems.

The upcoming chapter, Future of C# and .NET Core, deals with what's coming up, from features to trends and changes in the thriving .NET ecosystem, preparing you for what's in store down the line in the world of .NET developments.

15. C# and .NET Core Future

The development trend of the .NET ecosystem aids the introduction of new features, tools, and updates to developers for the creation of great applications. Future trends for .NET Core and C# will be impacted by cross-platform applications, cloud-native applications, machine learning, and the maximization of performance and productivity. This chapter elaborates on the foreseen developments in C# and .NET and emerging trends that will impact the future of application development.

15.1 The Road to .NET: From .NET Core Through to .NET 8 and Beyond

The transition from the .NET Framework to .NET Core and then to the unification of .NET was a migration to have cross-platform support with contemporary performance and more modern capabilities in development. The one unified platform, following .NET 5, takes all the best together into one combined feature set from .NET Core, .NET Framework, and Xamarin, allowing for development on many more platforms.

15.1.1 The Vision of .NET 8

NET 8 fulfills this vision by emphasizing cloud-native capabilities, performance, security improvements, and language features that enable modern development practices. Key objectives for .NET 8 and extend further to include:

Better Cloud-Native Support: Improved tools and libraries for developing cloud-native and microservices-based applications.

Performance and Efficiency: Industry-leading performance on runtime speed and memory efficiency.

Unified Developer Experience: Further simplifies the .NET ecosystem to make cross-platform and multi-device development more consistent.

Security: Brings advanced security features, directly onto the framework, to help developers build more secure applications.

.NET 8 will lay the foundation for subsequent releases that will continue to support cross-platform, developer productivity, and optimization of modern workloads.

15.2 C# Language Advancements

As C# has been developed over the years, it has provided features such as LINQ, async/await, pattern matching, and records. With C# 12, we're now witnessing efforts to simplify code, remove boilerplates, and support functional programming paradigms.

15.2.1 Language Features We Might See

While the specifics for each version can vary, here are some trends and features we might expect in the future for C#:

1. Better Pattern Matching:

Some recent editions of C# have included robust pattern-matching ability, allowing developers to write much more readable and expressive code. Future editions of C# are very likely to expand the functionality available in pattern matching, perhaps including new types of patterns or even more concise syntax.

Example:

```
public static string DescribeShape(Shape shape) => shape switch
{
    Circle(var radius) => $"A circle with radius {radius}",
    Rectangle(var width, var height) => $"A rectangle {width}x{height}",
    _ => "Unknown shape"
};
```

2. Advancements in Support for Functional Programming:

As functional programming is also on the rise in modern software development, C# may yet include features that promote immutability, expressions over statements, and even new constructs that belong to the family of functional paradigms.

3. Meta-Programming Advancements:

Meta-programming allows developers to write code that generates other code. This might also extend to even more source generator features that facilitate the generation of better, more boilerplate-free code during compile-time.

15.2.2 More Advanced Async Programming

Async programming is the bedrock upon which scalable applications are built. Further improvements will include more fine-grained management over the execution of asynchronous code and enhanced support for multithreaded, concurrent applications

Example:

```
public async Task ProcessTasksAsync(IEnumerable<Func<Task>> tasks)
{
    // Execute tasks concurrently with improved parallelism controls.
    await Task.WhenAll(tasks.Select(task => task()));
}
```

15.3 Cloud-Native Development

Cloud-native development, based on microservices, serverless architectures, and Kubernetes, is becoming the new normal for modern applications. .NET is adopting features and tools at a rapid pace to support cloud-native architectures.

15.3.1 Integration with Serverless Computing

Serverless computing allows for scalability and reduced management of infrastructures, while .NET has been more and more supported on platforms like Azure Functions and AWS Lambda. Future releases would probably enhance serverless support so .NET applications could benefit and use cloud resources even more intuitively and efficiently.

Example: Serverless Function in .NET with Dependency Injection

```
public class Function : IFunction
{
    private readonly IProductService _productService;
```

```
        public Function(IProductService productService)
        {
            _productService = productService;
        }


        [FunctionName("GetProduct")]
        public async Task<IActionResult> Run(
            [HttpTrigger(AuthorizationLevel.Function, "get", Route = "product/{id}")]
HttpRequest req,
            int id)
        {
            var product = await _productService.GetProductByIdAsync(id);
            return product != null ? new OkObjectResult(product) : new NotFoundResult();
        }
    }
```

15.3.2 Cloud-Native Optimizations and Tooling

In future versions of .NET, support for a number of tools that improve the developer experience when creating cloud-native applications will include:

CI/CD Integration Made Easy: Native tools for GitHub Actions, Azure Pipelines and other CI/CD platforms.

More tightly integrated Kubernetes and Docker to better leverage these for developing, deploying, and managing .NET containerized applications.

15.4 Cross-Platform and Multi-Device Development

The unified platform for the widest variety of devices and platforms: mobile (iOS, Android), desktop (Windows, macOS, Linux) and web (Blazor, WebAssembly). That will continue as .NET continues making it easier to write cross-platform applications from a single codebase.

15.4.1 MAUI and the Road for Multi-Platform Applications

.NET MAUI is Microsoft's promise of cross-platform UI development, so one code base can target Windows, macOS, iOS, and Android in parallel.

MAUI Future Enhancements: Wait for more platform-specific integrations, performance improvements, and simplified tooling within MAUI to let .NET developers work with true cross-platform applications.

15.4.2 Blazor and WebAssembly Advancement

Blazor Support for WebAssembly

WebAssembly has opened the door to running .NET applications right in the browser. Consequently, it enables developing powerful web applications without JavaScript.

Blazor Hybrid

The future of Blazor is embodied by Blazor Hybrid. It is a new variant that allows embedding Blazor components into MAUI applications. With it, you can build applications that can run both on desktop and mobile devices, sharing the codebase.

Example: Blazor Component in .NET MAUI

```
<ContentPage xmlns="http://schemas.microsoft.com/dotnet/2021/maui"
        xmlns:blazor="clr-
namespace:Microsoft.AspNetCore.Components.WebView.Maui"
        x:Class="MyApp.MainPage">
    <blazor:BlazorWebView HostPage="wwwroot/index.html">
        <blazor:BlazorWebView.RootComponents>
            <RootComponent Selector="#app" ComponentType="{x:Type
local:MyBlazorComponent}" />
        </blazor:BlazorWebView.RootComponents>
    </blazor:BlazorWebView>
</ContentPage>
```

This will allow you to easily weave together web technologies with native mobile and desktop capabilities, bringing even more versatility to this framework.

15.5 Machine Learning and AI in .NET

Machine learning and artificial intelligence are revolutionizing software applications. ML.NET is a tool set available from Microsoft for building machine learning models on top of .NET.

15.5.1 ML.NET and ONNX Support

ML.NET is a cross-platform, open-source machine learning framework for .NET. By supporting ONNX or Open Neural Network Exchange, developers can use pre-trained models created with frameworks like TensorFlow or PyTorch in their .NET applications.

Example: Using an ONNX Model in .NET using ML.NET

```
var modelPath = "model.onnx";
var mlContext = new MLContext();
var model = mlContext.Model.Load(modelPath, out _);

var predictionEngine = mlContext.Model.CreatePredictionEngine<InputData,
OutputData>(model);
var result = predictionEngine.Predict(new InputData { Feature1 = 1.0f, Feature2 =
2.0f });
```

ONNX integration enables .NET applications to take advantage of complex, high-performance ML models, making .NET a feasible platform for AI applications.

15.5.2 Integrating with External AI Services

Net applications integrate very easily with external AI services, including Azure Cognitive Services and OpenAI's GPT APIs, in natural language processing and computer vision and so on.

Example: Integrate Azure Cognitive Services for Image Analysis

```
var client = new ComputerVisionClient(new
ApiKeyServiceClientCredentials("<Your-API-Key>"))
{
    Endpoint = "<Your-Endpoint>"
};

var result = await client.AnalyzeImageAsync("https://example.com/image.jpg",
                        new List<VisualFeatureTypes?> {
VisualFeatureTypes.Description });
```

On top of that, it will include such services that allow developers to add capabilities of AI to NET applications without deep knowledge in machine learning.

15.6 Developer Productivity and Tooling Improvements

Improving the developer productivity remains the core focus in the evolution of .NET. Microsoft has been adding tools and libraries meant to simplify and accelerate development.

15.6.1 Hot Reload and Live Reload

Hot Reload allows developers to change code in running applications and view the effect of changes without restarting the application, although it does require a complete restart. This feature is still improving, handling more scenarios with even better feedback loops in development.

15.6.2 Better Debugging and Diagnostics

In the future, releases of .NET will be bringing about better debugging and diagnostic tools to go better into integration with dotnet-dump, dotnet-trace, and Visual Studio's Diagnostic Tools. The tools are good at enhancing the capability of developers to debug even applications in the production environment.

15.6.3 .NET Interactive Notebooks

.NET Interactive: Use of .NET with Jupyter Notebooks where developers can write C# code and run it interactively. Good for data exploration and even prototyping.

Use .NET Interactive for Data Analysis

```
#r "nuget: Microsoft.Data.Analysis"
using Microsoft.Data.Analysis;

var dataFrame = DataFrame.LoadCsv("data.csv");
display(dataFrame);
```

.NET Interactive allows testing of .NET code in a completely different way. It might be handy if you learn, experiment, or explore data.

15.7 Preparing for the Future of .NET and C# Development

As both .NET and C# continue to evolve, developers will want to:

Keep Current: Periodically update their codebase to leverage improved performance, new functionality, and security improvements within new versions of .NET and C#.

Learn about Cloud-Native Practices: Learn about cloud-native architecture, serverless computing, and containerization while these ideas continue to shape the "future" of .NET.

Expand AI and Machine Learning Skills: Learn ML.NET and the outside AI services to apply machine learning to applications.

Cross-Platform Development: Invest in MAUI, Blazor, and further cross-platform tools to develop applications that work across one or more devices and platforms.

Adopt DevOps and CI/CD Practices: As .NET seems to mesh tighter into CI/CD tools, adopting DevOps will enhance your deployment workflows.

15.8 Conclusion

This is just the future of .NET and C#-a future whose wave can be referred to as being wafting on all those exciting cloud-native optimizations, enhanced language features, seamless cross-platform development, MAUI, and Blazor. As the promises for improvements in the performance, productivity, and capabilities across platforms with .NET 8 and above come into play, developers will have the tools to build the next generation of applications. Keeping up with these trends and new practices, .NET developers can remain competitive and build robust, scalable, and innovative applications for the future.

That's all for this journey of C# 12 and .NET Core 8. With a solid foundation in .NET, you are well-set to take up modern software challenges and make use of the latest tools and techniques to write powerful, efficient applications in the years to come.

www.ingramcontent.com/pod-product-compliance
Lightning Source LLC
LaVergne TN
LVHW081757050326

832903LV00027B/1980